100 YEARS, 100 STORIES

George Burns

100 YEARS, 100 STORIES

WHEELER
PUBLISHING, INC.
ROCKLAND, MA

★ AN AMERICAN COMPANY ★

Published in Large Print by arrangement with
G. P. Putnam's Sons
in the United States and Canada.

Wheeler Large Print Book Series.

Set in 18 pt. Plantin.

Library of Congress Cataloging-in-Publication Data

Burns, George, 1896–
    100 years, 100 stories / George Burns.
      p.   cm.—(Wheeler large print book series)
    ISBN 1-56895-326-7 (hardcover)
    1. Burns, George, 1896– —Anecdotes. 2. Large type books.
I. Title. II. Series.
[PN2287.B87A3   1996a]
792.7'028'092—dc20
[B]   96-16955
                                              CIP

PREFACE

Here I am, starting my tenth and probably last book. I may even finish it. Then again, it may finish me.

I know what you're thinking: That can't be George Burns saying that. George Burns is an optimist. On his last special, didn't we all hear him say, "I've had a very exciting life. And I expect the second half to be just as exciting"?

You're right, I did say that. I also said, "When the Man knocks on your door, you have to go. When He knocks on my door, I'm not opening it." And then I said, "I'm going to stay in show business until I'm the only one left."

I did a lot of lines like that then, but that was before I fell backward in my bathtub and cracked my head open. Things haven't been the same since. Well, the bathtub is the same. But I'm not. That doesn't mean I'm giving up. Far from it. I'm still an optimist. But I'm not stupid. That nurse isn't watching me all day to see if my toupee is on straight.

Look, I'm not complaining. I still get to my office every day, still play a little bridge, still smoke my cigars, still can down a martini or two, and I have to say, I probably watch that nurse more than she watches me. I have lots to be grateful for. When I was singing with the Peewee Quartet ninety-three years ago, I couldn't have imagined the career I've had. It wouldn't have happened without Gracie. And it wouldn't have happened without all the loyal fans who stayed with me through the hits and the flops, the good jokes and the bad ones.

I can't put each of you in my will. I can't even thank you enough. But there is something I can do, and that's the reason for this book—to leave you with 100 of my best, funniest stories. That's one for each year. See, I can still count, too. When I've finished it, I hope it's a collection you'll enjoy not only now, but will want to go back to again and again for years to come.

George Burns
November 1995

One more thing: While I was writing that last paragraph, the nurse straightened my toupee.

ONE

To most people, a vacation is taking off from work and going someplace. That has never excited me. I don't mind going someplace, but I want to have a date to play when I get there.

So I'm still trying to figure out how I got talked into it, but on our fourth anniversary I found myself off work for three weeks and headed for Russia, via Paris and Budapest. There were three of us making the trip—myself, Gracie, and Jack Pearl's wife, Winnie, whom Gracie had invited to come along.

We crossed first-class on the *Ile de France*, and when we arrived in Paris, we checked into the George-V Hotel. Pretty classy for a guy with nothing booked.

On our first night in Paris, we decided to go to a Russian restaurant. You see, there's an old show-business tradition: If you do a new show, you break it in in New Haven before you bring it to New York. So we thought we'd better do the same thing with our stomachs. We'd break in the Russian food in Paris, and if we liked it, we'd take our stomachs to Russia.

It was a beautiful Russian restaurant, but when we sat down, I noticed the dinners cost fifteen dollars apiece. And believe me, in 1930 that was a fortune. So I said, "Girls, our dinner is going to be forty-five dollars without any tip. This place is too expensive for us." The girls agreed and started to order.

That's when the waiter asked, "Would you like to begin your dinner with a little caviar?"

I said, "Certainly we want a little caviar," and after he left, I turned to the girls. "What a question . . . do we want to begin our dinner with a little caviar? . . . For fifteen dollars I want not only caviar, I want a suit with two pair of pants to go with it."

I must admit the food was excellent, so we decided to take our stomachs with us to Russia—until the bill came. They had charged us an extra four dollars apiece for the caviar. That meant that dinner had amounted to nineteen dollars each. And I'm not going to tell you how much it came to with the tip or I'll start to cry again.

From there, like all good tourists, we went

to the Folies Bergères to see the world-famous nudes. In the middle of the show, with forty beautiful nude girls on the stage, Gracie leaned over to me and whispered, "George, it's a little shocking, isn't it?"

I whispered back, "Shocking! It's outrageous! I'll never eat there again!"

TWO

Fanny Brice was one of Broadway's biggest stars ever. She wasn't beautiful, but when she sang "My Man" in the Ziegfeld Follies she stopped the show. Later, on radio, she was a smash for years with her Baby Snooks character.

A few years before Fanny died I visited her in the hospital. She was very weak, confused, and forgetful. When I greeted her, she didn't even recognize me.

"Fanny," I said, "it's me, George Burns."

"I don't know any George Burns," she mumbled.

"We've been friends for forty years."

"Never saw you."

"Don't you remember?" I said. "We were on the same bill at the Shubert Theatre in Chicago."

"I never played Chicago."

"Of course you did, you were a sensation," I reminded her. "They were paying you $5,000 a week."

"It was $6,500," she whispered.

That she remembered.

THREE

A number of years ago I went to a classy party at Vincent Price's house. Now, Vincent Price was an art collector, and all his walls were covered with valuable paintings. He was very proud of his collection.

When he showed me around I thought I'd have a little fun and try to make him laugh. I pointed to a Rembrandt painting and said, "Vincent, that's a cute little picture. The kid who did that is probably going places."

He didn't laugh. He got very angry. "It's not a cute little picture, that happens to be a Rembrandt," he said, "and 'the kid' isn't going anyplace—'the kid' is gone!"

I said, "Oh, I'm sorry I missed him. What time did he leave?" That didn't get anything, either. Vincent slowly pulled open my breast pocket and poured his drink into it. I not only didn't get a laugh, but he ruined three of my cigars.

That night, every time I tried to get funny I got into trouble. I went over to Frank

Sinatra, who was at the bar having a drink. I said, "Frank, this is one of those magic moments in show business. Here we are at the same bar, drinking together—two of America's great singers." He kept staring at me, so I covered my pocket. But he moved over and poured his drink down my sleeve. By now I was getting pretty soggy.

I was seated at a very nice table, and my dinner partner was Shirley MacLaine. At the same table were the Jack Lemmons, the Walter Matthaus, and Dudley Moore. I never realized how short Dudley Moore was until I saw him dance with Dolly Parton. He looked like he had three heads. All I saw was the back of his neck, but I think he was smiling. She had to do the leading. I guess when he danced with her he couldn't see, because he ran into the wall twice. The orchestra was playing a wild rock number and Dudley was doing a waltz. I guess when he danced with her, he not only couldn't see but he couldn't hear.

So I went back to the bar, and George Hamilton was there. Jack Lemmon told me that George went out with three or four girls a night. Three or four girls a night! I'm lucky if I can hold on to my hair when the wind is blowing.

Well, I figured I did so well with Vincent Price and Frank Sinatra, why not make George Hamilton laugh, too? So I walked over to him and said, "George, I understand you're having a little problem getting a date. If you're not doing anything tomorrow night, I can fix you up with my sister Goldie."

He poured his drink down my cummerbund.

When I danced with Shirley MacLaine, I had to take very small steps, since everything I had on was shrinking. And after we danced, I said to Shirley, "That's a beautiful ruby you have in your belt buckle." It turned out to be the cherry from George Hamilton's cocktail.

And to make matters worse, when I drove home a policeman stopped me. I said, "Officer, what did I do?"

He said, "Nothing. I smelled you going by."

I said, "You'll never believe this story, but I just came from a party where Vincent Price, Frank Sinatra, and George Hamilton poured drinks all over me."

He said, "You're right. I don't believe the story."

I said, "Would you like to feel my cummerbund?"

Then he said, "Aren't you George Burns?"

I said, "Yes," and he said, "Wait until I tell my wife, Milly, that I ran into you. She's one of your biggest fans."

I said, "Good, maybe she'd like my autograph."

He said, "Like it? She'd love it. Put it right here on this ticket."

I must say I've had better nights.

FOUR

I've had many fine cinematographers film my movies, but I was never lucky enough to do a picture with James Wong Howe. He was one of the best cameramen in Hollywood, and this Chinese-American was acclaimed for his work on scores of films, including the classic *Casablanca*. He won several Academy Awards, including one for the Paul Newman picture *Hud*.

While he was under contract to Warner Brothers, he decided to open a Chinese restaurant on Ventura Boulevard, near the studio. He was always interested in Chinese cooking and thought it would be fun. When the restaurant was completed and the sign was hung, he hired a photographer to make a picture of the front of the place to use for advertising. The fellow, who didn't know who James Wong Howe was, kept going back and back to the edge of the curb, but he couldn't get the whole storefront in the picture. So he kept backing up into the street and dodging the cars that were speeding down the boulevard.

Wong walked out of the restaurant and saw what was happening. "Young man," he said, "why don't you just use a wide-angle lens, and then you can get the shot standing on the curb."

"Listen, mister," the photographer snapped, "you just stick to your noodles, I'll make the pictures."

AUTHOR'S NOTE

I made a mistake already. Those stories you've just read are good ones, but I shouldn't have started with them. They should have come later.

My problem is, I've told each of the hundred stories many times, but I've never had to arrange them. The stories about my parents and my early years should come first, then the ones about my vaudeville years should follow, and so on, down to the present.

I never realized that's the way to do it. But now I know. My nurse told me. So from now on, unless here and there I have a good reason for placing one elsewhere, the stories will come in chronological order. Chronological—that's her word, *not mine. Now I know what that means, too. How about that—a hundred years old and I'm still learning.*

FIVE

My father was a gentle, contented, religious scholar and a great provider. He provided my mother with twelve kids. That was it. How she managed to feed us all on what he'd bring in—correction, didn't bring in—will always be a mystery to me. Whenever he wasn't at his synagogue studying the Talmud, he'd be at some other small synagogue singing the services as a part-time cantor.

That didn't happen very often because his singing voice sounded a lot like mine. I remember one year he was asked to sing at a synagogue on Clinton Street for the High Holidays. This was a very poor little synagogue, so my father agreed to do it for nothing. That year, on the night when the period of fasting was over, all of us were gathered in the kitchen, waiting for dinner. My father was laughing and joking and teasing us kids; he seemed unusually elated. My mother didn't exactly share his mood because she was busy trying to water down a stew to the point where it would feed a bunch of kids who hadn't eaten in twenty-four hours. She looked at my father and said, "What are you so happy about? That synagogue is paying you nothing."

My father turned to her, and with a big, broad smile said, "I know, but they asked me to come back again next year."

Let's face it, my father was not handled by the William Morris Agency.

SIX

Unlike my father, my mother was a very practical lady. Nothing ever flustered her. No matter what the problem was, somehow she knew how to handle it.

A perfect example happened when I was seven years old. I was singing with three other Jewish kids from the neighborhood. We called ourselves the Peewee Quartet. Now, there was a big department store, Siegel & Cooper, that threw an annual picnic, and the highlight was an amateur contest with talent representing all the churches in New York. Right around the corner from where we lived was a little Presbyterian church. How it got in that neighborhood, I'll never know; it certainly didn't do big business.

Well, they had no one to enter in the contest, so the minister asked us four kids to represent the church. We jumped at the chance. So that Sunday, there we were, the Peewee Quartet—four Jewish boys sponsored by a Presbyterian church—and our

15

opening song was "When Irish Eyes Are Smiling." We followed that with "Mother Machree" and won first prize. The church got a purple velvet altar cloth, and each of us kids got an Ingersoll watch, which was worth about eighty-five cents.

Well, I was so excited I ran all the way home to tell my mother. When I got there she was on the roof hanging out the wash. I rushed up to her and said, "Mama, I don't want to be a Jew anymore!"

If this shocked her, she certainly didn't show it. She just looked at me and calmly said, "Do you mind me asking why?"

I said, "Well, I've been a Jew for seven years and never got anything. I was a Presbyterian for one day and I got a watch." And I held out my wrist and showed it to her.

She glanced at it and said, "First help me hang up the wash, then you can be a Presbyterian."

While I was hanging up the wash some water ran down my arm and got inside the watch. It stopped running, so I became a Jew again.

SEVEN

One summer, when I was seven years old, before I started singing with the Peewee Quartet, I hit upon the idea of going into the ice business. When it's hot, everybody needs ice.

I made myself a pull cart out of an apple crate and two old baby-buggy wheels. I nailed a stick onto the front to pull it, and I'd haul my cart down to an icehouse by the East River and buy a hundred-pound cake of ice for five cents. Then I'd pull it back to my neighborhood, split the cake into four quarters, and sell each one for five cents. I was making a fifteen-cent profit on every cake of ice. By hustling, I would be able to do this three times a day, which meant I could make a profit of $2.25 in a five-day week.

Unfortunately, I never made it to the end of the first week. In order to get to the icehouse I had to go right through the middle of this Italian neighborhood, and on the fourth day I was happily running along with my second cake of ice when these two rough-looking kids stopped me. Right away I knew I was in trouble when one of them said, "Hey, kid, I never saw you in this neighborhood! What's your name?"

I knew I had to come up with an Italian name, so I blurted out the only one I could think of: "Enrico Caruso!"

The bigger of the two stuck his face right in front of mine and snarled, "Are you Catholic?"

I looked right back at him and said, "Are you kidding? My father's a priest!"

That was the end of my ice business. They took my cart and my ice and chased me all the way back to Rivington Street.

EIGHT

My Uncle Frank was quite a character. During the Depression, he barely made a living running his butcher shop in Brooklyn. In those days, all the kids in the neighborhood were scurrying around, trying to make a few pennies.

One day a young boy came into Frank's store carrying a cat, and asked my uncle if he would buy it.

"Oh, no, I couldn't do that," Frank said. But then, noting the disappointment on the boy's face, he said, "But I'll take half a cat."

NINE

Years after my Uncle Frank's butcher shop went broke, he came to me one day and said he badly needed $750. I said, "Seven hundred fifty dollars? What for?"

"So I can die in Israel."

At least he had a good reason. I gave him the money and wished him well. Three years later, at a family reunion, who do I run into but Uncle Frank, looking happy and healthy.

"Frank," I said, "I gave you $750 so you could die in Israel."

"That's right, you did," he said. "And when I'm ready to die, I'll go to Israel."

TEN

When I was fifteen, my show-business career was going so badly that I took a job as an instructor at Bernstein's School of Dancing, which was surrounded by different ethnic neighborhoods on New York's East Side.

Being the newest instructor, I ended up having to teach the pupils no one else wanted. So I found myself dancing not only with a bunch of men, but with a bunch of big, awkward Polish, Hungarian, and Lithuanian men. It wasn't easy. But I must say, by the end of the course, they could do a pretty good fox-trot or two-step. The trouble was, they could do it only with me. And those Poles danced very close.

For some reason the owner, Benny Bernstein, thought he was a great businessman, and the biggest favor he could do for us would be to encourage us to follow his example. All day long we'd hear, "Watch and learn!" shouted in that heavy Jewish accent of his.

What a character! Every midnight, without fail, he'd stop the music to make this same announcement: "Ladies and gentlemen! Please remember we have dancing in this place Monday night, Tuesday night, Wednesday night, Thursday night, Friday night, Saturday night, Sunday night, and every night of the week!"

One night, when I'd been there almost a year, he rang a bell to make this special announcement: "Ladies and gentlemen! Two months from tonight we hold our annual masquerade ball. Once again, this ball is being held at Hennington Hall. Now, Hennington Hall is not a big hall. Stuyvesant Casino is bigger than Hennington. Hunt's Point Palace is bigger than Stuyvesant Casino. Webster Hall is bigger than Hunt's Point Palace. The answer is—the size of the hall has nothing to do with the ball. Sometimes in a big hall is a small ball. So the halls have nothing to do with the balls.

"Now, before the next dance I want to warn you again: Gentlemen are not allowed in the ladies' toilet."

After that one, I decided I'd watched and learned enough. So I danced my way out of there and back into show business.

ELEVEN

There were two fellows on the Lower East Side of New York, Maxie Reingold and Sidney Solomon. They went into vaudeville and called themselves Ryan and Sullivan, Singers, Dancers, and Roller Skaters. When they split up, I dropped Burns, became Sullivan, and went to work with Ryan. Then Sullivan got a new partner, and we did the same acts. So now you had Ryan and Sullivan and Sullivan and Ryan.

We split up again and we all got new partners. So now you had Ryan and Sullivan; Sullivan and Ryan; Ryan and Ryan; Sullivan and Sullivan.

Then we split up again. Now you had Ryan and Sullivan; Sullivan and Ryan; Ryan and Ryan; Sullivan and Sullivan; the Ryan Boys; and the Sullivan Brothers.

Before we were through, everybody on the East Side was named either Ryan or Sullivan.

There was one kid living there named Hymie Goldberg. He moved. He told me he was afraid to live in an Irish neighborhood.

TWELVE

Then I did an act with a seal: Captain Betz and Flipper. I was Captain Betz. With a seal you do really nothing. After each trick you just throw the seal a piece of fish. Well, anyway, Flipper and I were playing the Dewey Theater on Fourteenth Street, and that night I had a date with a very pretty girl. Her name was Betty McGrath.

I was ashamed to meet her, because after doing four shows a day with your pockets full of fish, you don't smell too good. But when I met her she never even noticed it. In fact, she complimented me on my aftershave lotion.

It turned out she did an act with Fink's Mules.

THIRTEEN

Before I teamed up with Gracie, I was pretty bad. I had to change my name every week. I couldn't get a job with the same name twice. I remember sitting in this small-time booking office and a theater manager came in and said, "Where can I find Maurice Valenti?" I said, "I'm Maurice Valenti." I thought I was.

He gave me a contract to play the Myrtle Theater in Brooklyn, and the contract read, MAURICE VALENTI AND HIS WONDER DOG. So I signed it. I'd do anything to stay in show business.

The next day I got myself a dog and went to the Myrtle Theater to do my act. I walked out on the stage with the dog under my arm. I stood there and sang my songs. In the middle of my third song the dog did his act . . . twice. It ruined my finish—I couldn't do my sand dance.

FOURTEEN

I once did a two-man act—Dunlap and Harris. I was Harris. Dunlap was the comedian, I was the straight man. A straight man does nothing but repeat things. The comedian would say something, then the straight man would repeat it and wait for the comedian to get his laugh.

I'd gotten so used to repeating things that one day when we hired a rowboat and went out fishing, Dunlap fell overboard and hollered "Help!"

So I repeated, "Help!"

While I was waiting for Dunlap to get his laugh, he drowned. He must have liked what he said because he came up, took three bows, and disappeared.

FIFTEEN

My straight-man pattern led to another bad experience. The one I just told you about ended only with my partner drowning. This one was more upsetting.

I had met a very pretty girl named Lily Delight, so I said, "How about you and me doing something together?" She said, "Sure," and invited me up to her apartment, locked the door, turned the lights down low, and said, "How would you like to have a drink?"

So I repeated, "How would you like to have a drink?" and she had one. Then she said, "Would you like to have another one?" I repeated, "Would you like to have another one?"

After the fourth drink, she said, "How about going into the bedroom?" So I repeated, "How about going into the bedroom?" Then she said, "How about turning out the lights?" So I said, "How about turning out the lights?" She turned out the lights, and I went home.

She wasn't getting any laughs, so I left.

SIXTEEN

Here's another story from my pre-Gracie vaudeville days. This one occurred at a time when I was doing even worse than usual. I not only couldn't keep a job, I couldn't keep a partner. So I was back doing a single, billed as "Harry Pierce, Singer from Rhode Island in an Act of Providence." The trouble was, the billing was better than my act. For three months . . . nothing. Then somehow I was booked into the Gem Theatre on New York's Lower East Side. I got a contract to play three days for fifteen dollars—five dollars a day—and the contract had a no-cancellation clause in it.

Well, after the matinee, when I came off the stage, the manager was waiting for me. He said, "Look, kid, that act of yours can close my theater. You're booked here for three days for fifteen dollars. Here's the fifteen—go home."

I said, "Not me. I'm booked here for three days, and I'm going to play the three days."

He said, "I'll give you twenty—go home."

I said, "All right, so you didn't like my first show. For the next show I'll change my songs. I'll open with 'Tiger Girl,' and then I'll sing 'In the Heart of a Cherry,' and then I'll do my big closing number: 'I'll Be Waiting for You, Bill, When You Come Back from San Juan Hill.'"

He said, "I'll make it twenty-five."

I said, "No, sir, I'm staying. I'm a performer. I've got cards printed."

He said, "Okay, kid, you can stay, but give me back your key to the men's room."

I did, but that was kind of bad, because that's where I was dressing. And let me tell you something: when you don't go to the men's room for three days it doesn't help your singing any. In fact, after the second day, I didn't dare do my yodeling finish.

SEVENTEEN

In my vaudeville days I was surprised to see how many performers hit the bottle. And when they overdid it, they didn't always know the condition they were in.

I was on the Pantages circuit one time with the monologuist Jack Whitehead and a dancing team called the Gliding Gascoynes. Gascoyne and Whitehead did a lot of drinking together. One night they got really bombed, and Gascoyne passed out in his dressing room. Whitehead sent for a doctor, who showed up immediately, and when Whitehead came out of the dressing room, I said, "How's Gascoyne?"

"Terrible," Whitehead replied. "The doctor asked him if he was seeing any pink elephants or green snakes, and Gascoyne said, 'No.' And the room was full of 'em."

EIGHTEEN

Looking back at my vaudeville career, I must say I was not exactly an overnight sensation. I tried everything. I even did a Spanish dancing act—José and Dolores. I was José.

Now, if I said this was the worst act in the world, I'd be lying. We weren't that good. I wore a Spanish outfit I'd bought at a store that specialized in secondhand costumes. It consisted of a gaucho hat, a ruffled shirt, a bolero jacket, black velvet pants, and flamenco boots. I got the whole outfit for $17. It would have cost $22.50, but the bolero jacket had a bullet hole in the back. And the pants were so big on me I had to wear a red sash to hold them up.

Now, Dolores was a pretty girl, except for one thing: she was very bowlegged. Every time she sat down, it looked as if somebody had stolen her cello. I would have said she looked like the entrance to a subway, but this is a classy book. Dolores was very self-conscious about her legs, so she had her costume made with a full skirt that came clear down to the floor. She was a great dancer, but nobody knew it. The audience was confused. They knew she was doing something under that skirt, but they didn't know what. I remember during one performance a fellow hollered up, "Hey, let me see your legs!"

Not to embarrass Dolores, I pulled up my pants and showed him my legs.

He hollered, "No, no, I want the girl to do it!"

And I said, "Why should she do it? They're my pants."

Anyway, besides that full skirt, Dolores wore a big heavy Spanish comb stuck in her hair. But this heavy comb pressed on a nerve in the back of her head, and it made her eyes bulge out. Our opening number was a fast Spanish fandango, and when we opened at the Colonial Theater in Schenectady and went into this fast dance, one of Dolores's shoulder straps broke and the left side of her dress fell down. And one of her things kept flapping against her chest. I thought it was the audience applauding, so I kept taking bows. When I saw what it was, I got so nervous that my sash broke and I lost my pants. And Dolores got so nervous that the comb popped out of her hair and her eyes fell in.

Well, there we were, Dolores with one of her things still applauding and her eyes in; me with a bullet hole in the back and my pants down. After the matinee they not only canceled us, they canceled Schenectady.

NINETEEN

When I was seventeen I started running around with a girl named Jean DeFore, who I thought was the greatest thing since ketchup. And you didn't have to hit her on the bottom to get her started. Jean DeFore was six years older than I was and, believe me, nobody would mistake her for Mary Poppins. At that time, if a girl wore a little bit of rouge, she was considered fast and loose. Well, Jean not only used rouge, she wore beaded eyelashes and lipstick. And to top it all off, she penciled in a black beauty mark on her cheek. All she needed was a red lantern hanging around her neck.

Jean may have been twenty-three when she had all that makeup on, but she looked more like thirty. But I was so proud that she'd got out with a seventeen-year-old kid that I couldn't wait to take her home to meet my mother. So one Sunday afternoon I did just that. As soon as we got in the door I said, "Mama, I want you to meet my sweetheart, Jean DeFore."

My mother was all smiles. "Sit down, Jean," she said, indicating a chair. "Make yourself at home." Well, we all got comfortable, and in a very friendly manner my mother asked Jean if she was Jewish. Jean said she wasn't, and then my mother inquired, "Do you understand Yiddish?" Again Jean said no. Turning to me and still smiling sweetly, my mother said in Yiddish, "Is this tramp planning to adopt you?" Then, looking directly at Jean, while speaking in her most motherly tone, she said, "I just told my son what a charming girl you are."

TWENTY

When I was in my early twenties, I played Philadelphia a lot. Every time I played Philadelphia I always stopped at a little hotel called the Hurley House. I'll never forget the Hurley House. All us small-time vaudeville actors stopped there. And there was a reason. Her name was Trixie Hicks, a very sexy waitress. Whenever you'd order breakfast, which consisted of donuts and coffee, Trixie would bring it up to your room. And she always stayed—she loved coffee. (I'm trying to keep it clean.)

Well, one morning I ordered breakfast, and when she brought it up, I said, "Trixie, how about a little coffee?" and she said, "I'd love to." Naturally, I locked the door. I didn't want the coffee to get cold.

Ten minutes later there was a knock on the door. And that was kind of bad, because I was right in the middle of my second cup. Let me tell you something. When I was in my twenties, I was good for three or four cups a night. And in the morning I had a little demitasse. Anyway, the guy knocking on the door turned out to be Hurley, the man who owned the hotel. He hollered, "Is Trixie Hicks in there?"

I got kind of panicky. I had an adjoining room with an actor named Jack Milo, so I knocked on Milo's door, Milo opened his door and I threw Trixie in. I let Hurley in. He looked around and couldn't find Trixie, so he left. Then I knocked on Milo's door, but he wouldn't give back Trixie. So I phoned downstairs to Hurley and said, "If you're looking for Trixie Hicks, she's in Jack Milo's room."

Hurley came up, knocked on Milo's door, Milo opened my door, and threw Trixie back. But this story has a sad ending. In the meantime my coffee got cold.

I love that story. There have been many times I wished I could enjoy coffee as much as I did when I was twenty-one.

TWENTY-ONE

During World War I, I was still a small-time vaudevillian, and some how I managed to scrape together enough money to get a ticket to a giant war bond rally at Madison Square Garden. George M. Cohan, Ed Wynn, and all the great monologuists, singers, and dancers of the day came out one after another in the huge three-hour show.

At that time the young Italian tenor Enrico Caruso was starring at the Metropolitan Opera House and was the toast of New York. When he came onstage toward the end of the program and sang two or three operatic numbers, he was an absolute sensation. For his final number he sang "The Star-Spangled Banner," and the audience gave him a five-minute standing ovation.

Al Jolson, who was scheduled to close the show, had to follow that. So out he came and, believe it or not, this was his opening line: "Folks, you ain't heard nothing yet."

Do you know something, he was right. Jolson got a longer ovation than Caruso.

TWENTY-TWO

To me, the funniest comedian ever was Charlie Chaplin, the biggest talent was Sammy Davis, Jr., and the greatest entertainer of all time was Al Jolson.

And that distinctive singing style of his—Jolson found that by accident. The night of one of his shows, he went to Lindy's Restaurant in New York for dinner, and had a double order of vegetables and sour cream. That happens to be a dish that consists of radishes, cucumbers, and onions. An hour later, while he was on stage singing "April Showers," he got a stomachache. He sang:

Though April showers——oooohhhhh
May come your way——oooohhhhh

And the audience loved it. And that was just from the radishes and cucumbers. When the onions hit him, he fell down on one knee, stayed there, finished the song, and turned out to be a sensation.

TWENTY-THREE

When I was about twenty-five, I used to hang out at a little restaurant called Wiennig and Sberber on Fifty-fifth Street in New York. I could get a full-course dinner there for thirty-five cents. When I wasn't working, they let me sign for the meal and run up my bill until I could pay it. One time I owed them $163, which should give you an idea of how well I was doing.

Wiennig's was a popular hangout for actors, prizefighters, song pluggers, and prostitutes. Some of them were very pretty, but it turned out they didn't give credit like Wiennig.

Wiennig and Sberber were a couple of real characters. Sberber never stopped talking, but nobody ever knew what he was talking about. One night Harry Richman came in for a late supper. Sberber came up to the table and said, "Mr. Richman, it's a pleasure to see such a talent eating here. I like music, too."

"You do?" Richman muttered.

"Do I like music?" Sberber went on. "I come from Chicago."

By now Richman was eating very fast. "I'm always at the opera," Sberber continued. "I've seen *Carmen* seventeen times. I know it by heart."

"You know *Carmen* by heart?" Richman asked, mildly impressed. "How does it go?"

Sberber said, "Good."

Wiennig was peculiar in a different way. He remembered only his last conversation. If you asked him a question, he gave you the answer to the last customer's question. One night I came in and said to him, "Have you seen Manny Mannishaw?" And he said, "Look on the floor, maybe it fell down."

Wiennig worked the cash register, checked out the kitchen, and waited on tables when the place was crowded. One night, when he was rushing around trying to do all three, a customer stopped him and asked, "Where's the men's room?"

Wiennig said, "Please, I've only got two hands!"

I'm still trying to figure that one out.

TWENTY-FOUR

In vaudeville you had to get off to a good start. So I always knocked my brains out trying to come up with a great opening. The first time Gracie and I worked together, this is what I came up with: I walked out onstage alone, stepped to the edge, leaned over to the orchestra leader in the pit, and said to him, "You see this little book? It tells twenty foolproof ways to meet girls."

He said, "Give me one way to meet a girl."

I said, "Okay. You take an impossible name like Mamie Dittenfest. Then you go up to a girl and say, 'Pardon me, aren't you Mamie Dittenfest?' She'll say, 'No.' You say, 'Well, you certainly look like her.' The next thing you know, you're buying her a cup of coffee."

At that point Gracie made her entrance. I said to the orchestra leader, "Watch this." Then I said to Gracie, "I beg your pardon, is your name Mamie Dittenfest?" And she said, "Yes."

It's what's known as a shock laugh. I was shocked that it didn't get one.

TWENTY-FIVE

That Dittenfest opening I just told you about lasted for one performance. In fact, that entire act lasted for one performance. In show business you have to learn from your mistakes. Fortunately for Gracie and me, that was one time I learned fast.

The way I had it, Gracie was the straight man . . . pardon me . . . the straight *person*. I was the comedian with the funny hat and the big bow tie that lit up and twirled around.

I noticed that the audience laughed at Gracie's straight questions, and my funny answers were greeted with loud silence, except for two or three, which got booed. It was obvious what I had to do. I stayed up all night rewriting the entire act and switching our roles. I became the straight man and Gracie became the comedienne.

And this time I got the opening right. Here is how it went: when Gracie and I, hand in hand, got to stage center, she glanced back to the side that we'd made our entrance from. There, standing just beyond the curtain, where the audience could see him, was a tall, good-looking man, motioning her to come over to him.

She dropped my hand, went to him, and he put his arms around her. They kissed, and he left. Gracie then returned to stage center, where I'd been standing and watching all this. When she got to me, she said, "Who was that?"

After waiting for the big laugh to die down, I said, "Gracie, you kiss a man and you don't know who he is?" And she said, "Mother told me never to talk to strangers."

Another tremendous laugh. More important, those two lines immediately set Gracie's character for the audience. They also became the pattern for the unique "illogical logic" underlying everything she would say from then on.

TWENTY-SIX

In vaudeville, trying out new material was always nerve-racking. One night Gracie and I did a routine for the first time that went over really big. It was about Gracie's brother going bird hunting, and this joke that Joe Frisco had given us got the biggest laugh:

GEORGE: What birds did he go hunting for?

GRACIE: Hepplewhites.

GEORGE: Hepplewhites? That must be a bird that came out this season.

GRACIE: No, the hepplewhite is a bird that flies backward.

GEORGE: Flies backward?

GRACIE: Yes. He's not interested in where he's going. He's only interested in where he's been.

The same night we received a wire from Fred Allen asking us to take the joke about the bird flying backward out of the routine. It was his joke. What a blow! If I took it

47

out, it would leave a hole big enough for a quartet to fall through.

I called Fred Allen and offered to buy it. I was willing to pay up to five hundred dollars for the joke, that's how much it was worth to us. But Fred wouldn't sell. He was in love with it, too.

At that time I was buying jokes from John P. Medbury. I called him in California and said, "I'm in a terrible spot. I've got to replace an important joke."

Medbury said, "What's the joke?"

I said, "It's about a bird that flies backward—it's not interested in where it's going, it's interested in where it's been."

Without hesitating a minute, he said, "Have the bird fly upside down, so if you shoot it, it falls up."

It got a huge laugh. I was so thrilled with it I sent Medbury $50 and thanked Fred Allen for saving me $450.

TWENTY-SEVEN

Wilton LaKye was one of the finest legitimate actors on Broadway, and like all the
other big stars of that time, each year he'd
play in vaudeville for five or six weeks. He
was headlining at the Keith Theater in
Cincinnati, and on the bill with him was a
little dancing act that opened the show.
They called themselves Dunbar and Dixon.

After Monday's rehearsal, LaKye went
into the bar next door to the theater to have
a drink. Dunbar and Dixon happened to
come in, and when they saw this big star,
Wilton LaKye, they almost jumped out of
their skins. They went over to their idol,
and Dunbar said, "Mr. LaKye, we just
wanted to tell you what a thrill it is for us
to play on the same bill with you."

LaKye said, "Thank you, boys."

Then Dixon said, "Mr. LaKye, we would
deem it an honor if we could buy you a
drink."

LaKye said, "I'm sorry, boys, but I'd just

as soon drink alone. I just got a wire saying that I lost my mother."

Dixon shook his head sadly and said, "We know just how you feel—our trunk is missing."

TWENTY-EIGHT

Novelty acts were very popular in vaude-ville, and there was one act that was really a novelty. This fellow worked with a chicken, and the chicken danced on one leg! The act was called Jackie Davis and Chick Fowler. The fellow's name was Chick Fowler.

Chick was a good entertainer, but he liked to drink a lot. Every once in a while he'd pour a little booze in a saucer for the chicken, and the chicken got to like it. He not only got to like it, he got to love it. Half of the time he was smashed. Well, it was tough enough for the chicken to dance on one leg when he was sober, but when he was smashed it was murder. Before you knew it, it got so they couldn't get a job.

I ran into Chick one day and said, "Chick, how are things going?"

He said, "Not good, George. Things are so tough that last night I pretty near ate my partner."

I said, "Chick, you wouldn't do a thing like that!"

He shook his head and said, "Of course not. But I must admit I ate the leg he wasn't using!"

TWENTY-NINE

The greatest bow for sustained applause was the one used by a tramp comedian who called himself Bilbo. He was a genius at pantomime, and the audience loved him. And this is how Bilbo finished his act.

Onstage he wore oversized yellow shoes with big rounded toes. When the curtain came down, Bilbo would stand in such a position that it would land on the tops of his shoes, leaving the toes extended in front so the audience could still see them. Then a baby spotlight would hit the shoes, and the audience would start to applaud. At this point Bilbo, behind the curtain, would step out of his shoes and go around and stand in the wings. Now, as long as the spotlight stayed on his shoes the audience kept applauding. Depending on his mood, when Bilbo thought the applause had gone on long enough, he'd step onstage in his stocking feet and take a bow. The audience realized they had been fooled and they loved him for it.

Unfortunately, this story also has a sad ending. Bilbo was finally booked into Hammerstein's, on Forty-second Street and Broadway, which was the Palace Theater at the time. He opened on a Monday and was never better. But what the audience didn't know was that Bilbo had a heart condition. At the end of that performance, when he stepped out of his shoes, he had a heart attack and died. The audience was wildly applauding his shoes, but Bilbo never came on for his last bow.

I don't know why I included this story. It's not exactly hilarious. But then, one out of a hundred isn't bad.

THIRTY

Vaudeville had many great monologuists. Of them all, Frank Fay would have to be considered the greatest. That's not just my opinion, it was his, too. He was also the most arrogant monologuist in vaudeville. You can make that the most arrogant performer in vaudeville.

One time he was testifying in court, and when the opposing lawyer asked him what his occupation was, he said, "I'm the greatest comedian in the world." Later, his own lawyer asked him why he would make a statement like that, and he said, "What could I do? I was under oath."

Besides being egotistical and arrogant, Frank had another endearing quality: he could be brutally sarcastic. And his sarcasm reflected his arrogance. When he put you down, it was as though he didn't even want to bother with someone so obviously beneath him.

Our paths first crossed when Gracie and I played the Palace. He had been the emcee there for months, doing the kind of job only Frank Fay could do. While we performed, he stood in the wings watching. After we finished the act, he sauntered over to us and, ignoring me, took Gracie's hand and began to tell her how impressed he was with everything about her—her unique delivery, her engaging personality, her delicate charm. He couldn't stop complimenting her. And then, still not giving me so much as a glance, he leaned toward her, and she leaned toward him, and he said, "But where did you get the man?"

There was only one Frank Fay. One was enough.

THIRTY-ONE

During the time I was doing the Burns and Allen show on radio, most of the variety shows were using big bands. Our band leader was Artie Shaw. When we moved the show from New York to California, Artie had a problem with James Petrillo, who was then head of the musicians' union. One of the key men in Artie's band was his trumpet player, and naturally Artie wanted to bring him along to California. But Petrillo wouldn't allow it. Artie was very upset because this trumpet player was extremely important to him, but Petrillo wouldn't give in.

The day after we arrived in California I was on my way to the Brown Derby restaurant to have a drink, and there on the newsstand was a headline that read, "Lana Turner Divorces Artie Shaw." There was a picture of Lana in a sweater, and she looked absolutely beautiful. Inside the Derby, there was Artie at the bar, having a drink. I knew how bad he must have felt about losing a beautiful girl like Lana, so I put my arm around him and said, "Artie, don't take it too hard. Things like that happen to everybody."

Artie looked at me and said, "To hell with Petrillo. I'll find myself a trumpet player out here!"

THIRTY-TWO

When Gracie and I were doing radio, we hired Tony Martin as our singer. At that time Tony was very young and had been working as a saxophone player with a small band in Oakland. He sang with a saxophone around his neck, and he'd always play with the buttons on the sax while he was singing because he didn't know what to do with his hands.

When he came on our show he was just a singer and didn't need the saxophone. On his first show he sang "Begin the Beguine," and he was so used to playing with his buttons that when he got to the second chorus, he lost his pants.

THIRTY-THREE

John P. Medbury was about five feet five, must have weighed 250 pounds, and was never stuck without a doughnut or an answer. Before he came to work for me as my head writer, he was writing two syndicated humor columns in an office in the Hollywood Plaza Hotel. Working for him was an ambitious young fellow named Frank Williams.

I should explain that besides writing and eating, Medbury would entertain certain young ladies in his office from time to time.

Well, one day Mrs. Medbury happened to drop in, and while looking for a stamp, she opened the top drawer of Medbury's desk, and there was a pair of black lace panties. Gingerly holding them up, she looked at Medbury and said coldly, "John, what are these doing here?"

Without batting an eye, Medbury angrily called into the other office, "Frank, get in here!"

The bewildered young writer walked in,

and Medbury threw the panties at him, saying, "Give these back to your girl. You're fired!"

On her way out, Mrs. Medbury stopped at Frank's desk and said, "Frank, you're not fired. And tell lover-boy it didn't work. He's not as fast as he used to be."

THIRTY-FOUR

Medbury was one of several writers I had in radio. Later on, when we did our TV show, I remember hiring a very good team of writers named Seaman Jacobs and F-F-F-Fred F-F-F-Fox. I write it that way for two reasons: Fred stuttered, and he never stopped joking about it himself. On the other hand, his partner, whom everyone called Si, was very articulate. What made no sense was that at our meetings it was Freddie who did most of the talking, and when it came to reading one of their five- or six-page story lines, it was F-F-F-Freddie who always p-p-p-plowed through it. Once, when I was alone with Si, I asked him, "Si, you could read those story lines in one-tenth the time it takes Freddie. Why do you have him do it?"

Si said, "George, the way Freddie talks, he needs all the practice he can get."

Well, I couldn't argue with that, so every Monday morning Freddie would come in and read the story line. One morning he was going along as usual when he came to a scene that he got very enthused about. In his excitement he read through the entire scene without once stuttering. When he finished, I said, "Freddie, do you realize that you just read three pages without stuttering?"

Freddie's eyes widened and he jumped up, shouting, "My God, I'm c-c-c-cured!"

THIRTY-FIVE

I've always been patient with stutterers. Maybe that's because one of my early vaudeville partners, Billy Lorraine, stuttered so badly that it would take him five minutes to say "Come in." The poor guy could never get out any of the spoken lines in our act, but for some reason he had no problem when he sang.

Once, when we were playing the Pantages Theater in Los Angeles and living at the Continental Hotel, I went out to get my hair cut. In those days I had some. When I got back to the hotel, Billy rushed up to me, all excited. I could see he had news for me.

"W-w-w-w . . ."

"Yeah, yeah, go on, Billy."

"W-w-w-w . . ."

He couldn't go on. I said, "Okay, start over."

Again: "W-w-w-w . . ."

"We got a job?" I took a shot—*we* starts with a *w*.

He shook his head negatively.

"So what is it, Billy?" I pleaded.

Again: "W-w-w-w . . ."

I said, "Sing it, Billy, sing it!"

And clear as a bell, he sang, "We were just robbed."

THIRTY-SIX

For those of you who may not remember him, Joe Penner was a burlesque comic who graduated to radio and at one time had a top-rated radio show. He was the first one to ask, "Wanna buy a duck?" and he asked it so often on his weekly show that it caught on and became a nationwide catchphrase.

During one of our summer breaks, I took Gracie and our two kids, Sandy and Ronnie, to Hawaii for a week's vacation. Staying at the same hotel were the Penners and two other couples that we knew. Every day we sat around together at the beach, and although Gracie got the laughs when we performed, I was the one who had to keep our little group in stitches. I kept waiting for Penner to come up with something—a story, a topper, a funny line, a dirty joke. Nothing. Not a snicker all week.

The last day, going up in the elevator in our hotel, this top comedian said to me, "I'm never funny in the summer."

THIRTY-SEVEN

This story involves a big comedian who for many years had one of the most popular shows on radio. In person he was very funny and very fast on the uptake. But because I, like many of us here in Hollywood, know that he was also an incurable womanizer, I won't reveal his name. The tabloids would, but I have higher standards. I'll just tell you that his weekly half-hour show took place in a New York tavern.

Anyway, this comedian got married to a very lovely lady, and the newlyweds immediately went on a honeymoon cruise. And right away, the first night out, he wound up in the cabin of another woman. After a few hours the wife went looking for him, and sure enough, she bumped into him just as he was coming out of the other woman's cabin. And without batting an eye, he said to her, "I forgot to tell you, I'm also a jewel thief."

THIRTY-EIGHT

There was a young fellow around Hollywood named Barney Dean who used to amuse the performers with his little jokes and stories. Bob Hope took a particular liking to him and always had him hang around with him in his dressing room. Bob kept him on salary just to keep him company, and in order to get a deduction he listed Barney as a writer.

Once, when I was set to do a guest spot on the Hope radio show, I called Bob and asked him to get a script to me. He said he would have a messenger drop it off that afternoon.

The next thing I knew, the script was delivered to me, and the messenger was Barney Dean. "Barney," I said, "how come you're the messenger? You're a writer!"

"George," he said, "if I wasn't a messenger, I wouldn't be a writer."

THIRTY-NINE

I've always said there are only two comedians who made me laugh when I just looked at them. One was W. C. Fields. This story is about the other one—Ben Blue.

Shortly before we came to Hollywood, Gracie and I took a six-act vaudeville unit out on a tour of eight weeks, and Ben Blue was one of the acts. We got a $10,000 guarantee from each theater, out of which we paid each of the acts, and if the box-office receipts were over a specified amount, the theater and Burns and Allen would split the difference. So if business was good we could make quite a bit of money.

We were doing four shows a day to capacity crowds, but we would do even better if we could just squeeze in an extra show. However, the only way that could be done was to cut Ben Blue's act from thirty-five minutes to thirteen minutes. And I'll tell you a little secret: It's very difficult to cut an actor, especially Ben Blue. Because as much as the audience loved Ben Blue's act, Ben Blue loved it even more. Now, at that time I was paying Ben Blue $750 a week, so I called him into my dressing room and said, "Sit down . . . have a drink . . . here, smoke a cigar. . . ."

"You can't cut my act," he broke in.

"Ben," I said, "now that you've brought it up, let me tell you something. You're getting $750 a week and you're doing thirty-five minutes. If you cut your act down to thirteen minutes, we'll be able to do an extra show and I'll give you $1,000 a week. You'll be making $250 a week more."

He stood up and indignantly said, "Who the hell do you think you're talking to? Thirteen minutes! That would mean I'd have to take out the 'Ten Cents a Dance' bit that I do with my wife, and that's the only thing she does in my act. If I cut that, she'd divorce me!"

I said, "Ben, forget it, I'm sorry I brought it up."

With that, he stormed out of the room. I didn't even have time to powder my nose before he stuck his head back into the room and said, "Three hundred fifty dollars?"

"You got it," I said.

So we did five shows a day, Ben did thirteen minutes, and two weeks later his wife divorced him. Isn't that a good story? But wait, there's more. His wife took him to court and sued him for $600 a month alimony. At the trial Ben defended himself. He said to the judge, "Your Honor, I can't afford to pay my wife $600 a month alimony. If I did that, I wouldn't have enough money to put gas in my Duesenberg."

The judge stared at him and said, "You've got a Duesenberg?"

There was a pause, then Ben quickly said, "But, Your Honor, don't forget, I drive it myself."

The next time I saw Ben Blue he was driving a Chevrolet.

FORTY

In 1932, when Gracie and I signed a two-year contract with Paramount to make feature pictures, the first thing we had to do was move to Hollywood. And the first mistake we made was to ask Gracie's sister to find us a house.

She not only found us a house, she found us an Italian villa on four and a half acres. It was so big we didn't have any next-door neighbors. And the house was huge, with dozens of enormous rooms. We spent most of our time in the kitchen because that was the only room that didn't have an echo in it.

It was located on Sunset Boulevard, right in the middle of Beverly Hills. I had a chance to buy the whole thing, house and lot, for $80,000. But I wasn't going to let them put anything over on me, so I just leased it for two years.

What we did buy was a big car. It was an extra-long, custom-built limousine with a glass partition between the driver and the passengers. We didn't buy this car to keep up with the Joneses—we got it to keep up with the house. But we had a problem with the car. The backseat was so deep that when Gracie sat down her feet didn't touch the floor. One day she said to me, "George, return the car and have them take six inches off the backseat."

I said, "Gracie, you can't do that. This car is designed by experts who get millions of dollars just to design backseats. This back is custom built."

"Well, mine isn't," she said.

There was a long pause, then I got very mad . . . because I hadn't thought of that line. But Gracie had won her point. We sent the car back and had six inches cut off the backseat. From then on, Gracie was very comfortable, but when anyone else sat down on that seat they fell on the floor.

FORTY-ONE

It wasn't long after Gracie and I began doing movies that the party invitations started to roll in. One of the first big ones we went to was given by the head of Paramount Studios. It was an engagement party for Gary and Rocky Cooper. The invitation was for eight o'clock, so of course, we showed up at eight o'clock. I guess that was our vaudeville training. In vaudeville, if you didn't show up on time, somebody else sang your songs.

Well, we arrived at eight o'clock sharp, and as we drove through the gate we were greeted by five little barking dogs. One of the parking attendants took our car, a butler let us in, and there we were, alone in this big living room that could hold at least 150 people. We both were served a martini, and I sat there looking at Gracie and she sat there looking at me. After about fifteen minutes of this I said to one of the butlers, "Where's the host?"

He answered, "Oh, he asked me to wake him at eight-thirty."

Ten minutes later, Gracie, who never drank, started to feel the effect of that martini. She left me, went into the powder room, put all the towels on the floor, and lay down and went to sleep. Now I was really alone, so I went outside and barked harmony with the dogs.

Eventually the guests arrived, and we had a fine time. Driving home that night, Gracie asked me, "Did you make any new friends?"

"Yeah," I said, "I met a cocker spaniel with a great sense of humor."

But that experience did teach us an important lesson about Hollywood parties: Don't arrive on time. The bigger the star, the later he gets there. In fact, we went to one party where Clark Gable was so late he never even showed up.

FORTY-TWO

Remember John P. Medbury, the writer who starred in two of my earlier stories? Well, he gave the craziest party Gracie and I ever attended. Maybe it was that way because he gave it in honor of Olsen and Johnson, the screwiest of screwball comedy teams.

Medbury lived in a big house in the Hollywood Hills, and when you arrived you parked your car and walked about a hundred yards up a roadway to the house. Well, this night when we arrived there were no attendants to take your car, but instead there were four donkeys tied to a tree. So after we parked the car, we carefully stepped around the donkeys and headed for the house. At the entrance to the roadway we had to go through a tent. Inside, there was a man sitting on a toilet reading a newspaper. Without even looking up, he said, "Keep walking, you're headed in the right direction."

A little farther on, there was a man sitting

in a big tree with a rifle. As we passed by he yelled, "This is private property. Don't pick any of the oranges!"

By the time we recovered from this, we were passing the garage. The door was open and the interior had been converted into a gaudy bedroom. Over the door was a red light, and beneath it stood a sexy girl soliciting business. In ten yards we had gone from private to public property.

Finally we reached the house, and there to greet us was John Medbury and a charming lady, whom he introduced as his wife. As I passed her she gave me a friendly little goose. And remember, this was in the 1930s, when this gesture wasn't socially acceptable. As soon as we walked inside, the butler came up to me and asked if he could borrow my matches. He said he had some candles to light. So I gave them to him. Later on I found out that he had done this to everyone. There were two hundred guests without matches. At first, this didn't seem to be a problem because there were plenty of matches lying around. However, they were trick matches. The minute you'd light them they'd go out. Wherever you looked, there was somebody trying to light a cigarette. This was one of the things I couldn't figure out. The girl under the red light, that I understood.

Here are a few more highlights of the evening: The party took place in July, but there was a fully decorated Christmas tree with presents underneath it in the living room. And there was a big fat Santa Claus sitting there with a cane. Every time somebody would try to pick up a present, Santa would say, "Ho, ho, ho," and whack him with the cane.

Every half hour a kid dressed like a bellboy would walk through the room, calling out, "It is now eight o'clock!" It was always eight o'clock, it never got any later.

The ladies' powder room was bugged, and anything that was said in there could be heard over speakers placed throughout the house. We heard one lady say, "What a stupid party. When the hell do we eat?" Then Medbury's voice came over the speakers, answering, "We'll eat when I'm damned good and ready!" I never did find out whether Medbury was in the ladies' room or with us.

At about ten o'clock at night, Medbury introduced a Russian man dressed in full diplomatic attire, complete with a red sash, and wearing more medals than Georgie

Jessel. He got up and spoke for fifteen minutes in Russian and left.

Finally, at eleven o'clock, they served a beautiful and elegant sit-down dinner. About an hour and a half later, a twelve-piece orchestra came in. They put up their music stands, took out their music, and tuned up their instruments. After a few minutes of this, the leader raised his baton, and the orchestra played a loud fanfare. With that, Medbury stood up and proclaimed, "Ladies and gentlemen, the party's over." The musicians packed up their gear and left. And so did the guests. When Gracie and I went through the tent the guy was still there, only now he was reading the morning paper.

FORTY-THREE

One of the really great funnymen of the twentieth century was W. C. Fields. He had a funny face and a voice to match, and he kept Broadway and motion-picture audiences laughing for decades. He also had a reputation as a drinker, both on and off the screen. He always wore a specially made vest with pockets that held small bottles filled with martinis. I invited him over to have dinner with Gracie and me one night, and when he came into my bar I had the gin, vermouth, olives, and ice lined up for him. He went to the door, removed his vest, and hollered to his chauffeur, "Clarence, my good man, you may take this vest. I'm getting my libations from another source."

In his early drinking days he went to his doctor for a checkup, and the doctor told him that if he didn't give up drinking, he would have only six months to live. Twenty years later, still drinking heavily, he went to another doctor, at the urging of all his friends. This doctor told him that if he didn't give up drinking, he would have only six months to live.

"You must be a very good doctor," Fields told him. "Twenty years ago another doctor made the same prediction."

W. C. Fields and I were good friends until this great comedian passed away. But we didn't actually meet until Gracie and I came out to Hollywood to make our first film for Paramount. It was called *International House*, and in the movie Gracie and Fields did a scene in which she played a waitress. She had the last line in the scene and then left, leaving Fields sitting there. Fields wanted to finish the scene with a funny line or a piece of business, but nobody could suggest anything that seemed to work.

Then I had an idea. "Look," I suggested, "you've got a cup of coffee, a glass of water, and a martini on the table. As soon as Gracie leaves, why don't you drop two cubes of sugar in the water, stir the coffee, and drink the martini?"

Fields stared at me for a minute or two, and then said in that peculiar drawl of his, "This is the first time I've ever liked a straight man."

FORTY-FOUR

One of the first feature movies Gracie and I appeared in was a big musical. Besides us, the cast included Bing Crosby, Bob Hope, Edgar Bergen, Jack Benny, Martha Raye, Betty Grable, Edward Everett Horton, and Jackie Coogan, plus about thirty chorus girls. The script looked pretty good, too. So everyone thought we were going to have ourselves a hit.

What we didn't realize going in was that the picture had a problem even bigger than its cast. The problem was, of all things, the producer. He wasn't too bright to begin with, which ordinarily wouldn't have mattered too much, but he was making a play for the lead dancer in the chorus, so he was always on the set. He was producing, directing, rewriting—anything to impress this girl he had the hots for.

One day he caused so many delays that it wasn't until nine o'clock at night that they were ready to shoot the big production number that had been scheduled for seven

A.M. As the cameras started to roll, he jumped up and hollered, "Cut!" and everything came to a halt. "I don't like the way the girls' legs look in those white tights," he said. "Put them all in black tights."

"But we don't have any black tights," the wardrobe woman protested.

"Then dye these black!" he ordered. "I'm tired of making all these decisions!"

"Look, if we wait for those tights," the director pointed out, "we won't be able to shoot this until tomorrow. It'll cost a fortune."

Ignoring him, the producer said, "Wrap it up, boys. We'll shoot this in the morning." And for the benefit of the lead dancer, he announced, "When I make a movie, money is no object."

Crosby, Hope, Benny, Bergen, all of us just looked at one another. We couldn't believe what was happening. The next morning we shot the number with all the girls in black tights. The white tights looked better.

There were another three days' worth of shooting, which took us two weeks to complete. The final scene was where Bob Hope and Martha Raye got married, and we were all down at the railroad station waving good-bye to them as they left for Niagara Falls on their honeymoon. We all thought that was it until the producer said, "Wait, I just thought of a great ending. As the train pulls out, all you stars lock arms and walk into the camera."

For the first time I thought he made a little sense, until I noticed I was locking arms with Martha Raye, and next to her was Bob Hope. I went over to the producer and quietly pointed out, "Look, Bob and Martha can't be in the finish. They're not here, they're on the train to Niagara Falls."

"Forget it," he said. "Nobody is going to notice those little technicalities."

So we all locked arms and walked into the camera. That was the finish of the picture, the finish of the producer . . . and almost the finish of a lot of acting careers.

FORTY-FIVE

When I made one of my early movies, we had a young actor with us who drove the director crazy. He was a method actor, and he needed a motivation for everything he did. He wouldn't move unless he knew why he was moving.

There was this one scene where he had to go to the bathroom. He asked the director why he was going to the bathroom.

The director said, "For the same reason everybody goes to the bathroom."

The actor said, "We better not do that scene, because it won't be believable. I don't have to go to the bathroom."

The director stared at him. "Pretend you had breakfast and then go to the bathroom."

The actor said, "Should I pretend I had a big breakfast or a small breakfast?"

After a long pause, the director said, "What difference would that make?"

He said, "I want to know how long to stay in the bathroom."

The director said, "Forget the bathroom, you won't be able to get in."

He said, "Why not?"

The director said, "Because the actor who's taking your place will be in there."

That was the end of the method actor. From then on, I didn't take any chances. Whenever the director looked at me, I went to the bathroom.

FORTY-SIX

Not many people know that longtime chairman of the board of Paramount Pictures, Adolph Zukor, and I were very close friends. I'm not sure that even Zukor knew it. But Gracie and I did make about a dozen pictures for him. And I would often go into his office and play gin rummy with him.

We were playing one time, and he knocked and said, "I'm going down with ten." But he had eleven—he had a seven and four.

I said, "Before we throw the cards in, Mr. Zukor, you know Gracie and I are now doing this picture with Bing Crosby, and in it Crosby sings five songs. How about letting me sing one of those songs?"

He looked right at me and said, "George, Bing Crosby, one of our major stars, is going to sing all five songs."

So I looked back at him and said, "Mr. Zukor, you got eleven."

He said, "George, you and Gracie have

been with us now for six years. Do you like working for Paramount?"

"I love it."

"Do you like living out here?"

"I love it."

"You wouldn't want to move back east?"

"No, sir."

Then he said, "How much is seven and four?"

I said, "Ten."

Bing Crosby sang the five songs, Gracie and I never moved back east, and I never won a game of gin rummy from Mr. Zukor.

FORTY-SEVEN

Samuel Goldwyn was one of Hollywood's great producers, and some of his films were classics. However, he was quite a character, and his fractured English brought on a series of expressions that were to become known as Goldwynisms. In the old days, lines like "Quick as a flashlight" and "An oral contract isn't worth the paper it's written on" were told and retold all over Hollywood.

Goldwyn was jealous of the success MGM had with Greta Garbo and decided to duplicate it by signing a beautiful Russian actress named Anna Sten and starring her in a film of Emile Zola's *Nana*. He went to the successful writer Edward Chodorov and asked him to write the screenplay, but Chodorov turned him down. He thought it was a weak idea and wouldn't make a good motion picture. For an hour Goldwyn tried to persuade him to work on the picture, but Chodorov refused, again warning Goldwyn not to make it.

Well, Goldwyn went ahead, spent a fortune on the film, and went overboard on the advertising campaign, with twenty-four-sheet billboards all over the United States selling "Anna Sten in *Nana*."

The picture turned out to be Goldwyn's biggest flop, bombing in every theater it played, and Sam steamed about it for a year. When he started planning his next film, an agent suggested that Edward Chodorov would be the perfect writer to do the screenplay.

"Chodorov!" Goldwyn exploded to the agent. "Never! He was associated with my biggest flop!"

FORTY-EIGHT

One of my very close friends, Eddie Buzzell, was one of our top motion-picture directors. He directed many movies, including *Honolulu*, the last motion picture Gracie and I made. Eddie told me a story that I think is worth passing on. When he first came to Hollywood he went to work for Columbia Pictures. At the end of his first year he had a verbal agreement with Harry Cohn, who was the president of the company, to get a $250 weekly raise. Now, I'm not going to say that Harry Cohn was a hard man to do business with—I don't have to, everybody else has said it. When the year was up, Eddie went into Cohn's office and asked for his raise. Cohn turned on his charm. He said, "Eddie, Sam Briskin is right across the hall. He's head of production, so go in and ask him for the raise. If he okays it, it's certainly all right with me." Cohn stood up and put a fatherly hand on Eddie's shoulder. "You know me, Eddie," he continued, "when I make somebody a promise, it's a promise."

So Eddie went across the hall. When he walked into Briskin's office Sam wasn't there, but the intercom was buzzing. Eddie pushed down the lever and said, "Yeah?"

Cohn's voice came over the intercom. "Sam, Buzzell is on his way in there to ask for a raise. Don't give it to him."

Eddie pushed down the lever just as Sam walked in. Sam said, "What can I do for you, Eddie?"

Trying to act nonchalant, Eddie said, "I just left Harry Cohn's office. I'm due for a raise, and he said if it's all right with you, it's all right with him."

"Well, he's the boss," Sam said. "If it's all right with him, you've got it."

Eddie Buzzell stayed with Columbia Pictures for years and got many raises, but Harry Cohn never knew that Eddie was always $250 ahead of him.

FORTY-NINE

When Harry Cohn was the president of Columbia Pictures, he made lots of movies, but very few friends, and even fewer admirers. He browbeat producers, directors, actors, and he used to run through the writers' building every night after six, turning off the lights and yelling, "When not in use, turn off the juice!" There was no tougher studio head in town.

After his funeral, the studio gave a giant memorial service for him on their biggest soundstage. All the Columbia employees and hundreds of Hollywood celebrities showed up for the service. Danny Kaye and I went there together. When we arrived, the giant stage was jammed to capacity. Danny looked at the huge crowd, then turned to me. "See, George," he said, "give them what they want and you can't keep them away."

Then there was Lee Mortimer, the widely read show-business columnist for the old *New York Mirror*. Unlike Harry Cohn, Lee had lots of friends, but Frank Sinatra wasn't one of them. He resented the kind of publicity he was getting from time to time in Mortimer's column. One time, when he thought Lee had gone too far, Frank took a punch at him, a punch that made the front pages all over the country.

Now a nationwide figure, Lee became noted for two things: One was the way he always referred to death. He called it "taking a cab." You never read in his column that this celebrity or that one died; it was always "so and so took a cab."

The other thing that became common knowledge about Lee was his love for anything Chinese. He loved Chinese food, Chinese art, Chinese furniture, Chinese clothes, and most of all, Chinese women.

These two unusual traits were so well known that when Lee died, another Broadway columnist wrote, "Today our friend and colleague, Lee Mortimer, took a rickshaw."

FIFTY

The Barrymores—Ethel, Lionel, and John—were America's royal family of the legitimate theater. No other family came close. Even my family of twelve brothers and sisters wasn't in it.

Of the three Barrymores, John probably had the most distinguished record on the New York stage. His performances in *Hamlet* and many of Shakespeare's other plays compared favorably to those of England's greatest Shakespearean actors.

One time, when he got into a cab in New York City, the driver, who was Jewish and spoke with an accent, said, "It's a pleasure to have you in my cab, Mr. Barrymore. I recognized you immediately."

"How good of you," Barrymore replied.

As they drove along, the driver asked what he was doing in New York.

"I am here to appear in Shakespeare's *King Lear*," Barrymore informed him.

The driver was impressed. *"King Lear,"* he said, "I must have seen it a dozen times.

I've seen it played by all the great actors: Jacob P. Adler, David Kessler, Boris Tomashevsky, Maurice Schwartz." Then he thought a second. "Tell me something, Mr. Barrymore, do you think it'll go in English?"

That line wasn't what drove him to Hollywood, but Barrymore did have quite a movie career. One of his early films was *Morning Glory*, which was also one of the early films for his co-star, Katharine Hepburn. From the day shooting started, the two didn't get along. They interrupted the filming of numerous scenes with shouting scenes of their own. When the picture was over, Hepburn went to Barrymore's dressing room and said, "Mr. Barrymore, I'll never act in another picture with you."

Barrymore looked down at her, and with a very sweet expression on his face, said, "Miss Hepburn, you never have."

FIFTY-ONE

There was a little agent named Charlie Gold, long gone now, who had a tiny office outside fashionable Beverly Hills. One day he went to a Dodger baseball game and by chance found himself seated next to Clark Gable. During the game they started to talk, and before long they were getting along famously.

At that time Clark happened to be thinking about changing agents, so when Charlie mentioned that he was an agent, Clark said to him, "Why don't I drop over to your office tomorrow and we'll have a talk." That was very exciting to Charlie, except for the thought of Clark seeing his crummy little office. So he immediately said, "Clark, why should you bother? I'll be glad to come to your house." But Clark insisted on going to Charlie's office, and they set the time.

When Clark arrived, he took a long look at the office and at the little old secretary sitting at the little old desk that Charlie shared with her. Then, sitting in the only extra chair, he said, "You know, Charlie, I like this kind of an office—plain, simple, nothing ostentatious. I like the way we seem to interact, and I think we'd make a good team. Tell me . . . are you Jewish?"

Charlie hesitated for a moment, and then said, "Not necessarily."

FIFTY-TWO

Except for replacing Fred Clark with Larry Keating, I made only one major addition to our TV cast during its entire eight-year run. That was when I had our son, Ronnie, join the show. It turned out to be a very good move. He did a great job. And why not? He was playing himself . . . our son, Ronnie Burns, who was always on the lookout for a new girlfriend. It was a part he knew by heart.

I still think Ronnie could have made it in show business. He had a nice relaxed manner, he was tall and good looking, and had all the instincts of a good actor. I even offered to send him to New York to study under Lee Strasberg at the Actors Studio, where some of our biggest stars came from. But Ronnie turned it down; he said he would miss all the girls at the Luau Restaurant.

I said to him, "Ronnie, they have restaurants in New York that also have pretty girls. And the pretty girls in New York have the same thing that the pretty girls have in California, and in the exact same spot." He appreciated this lesson in sex education. In fact, he called from the Luau that night to thank me.

But I never did quite understand why Ronnie wasn't in love with show business. On our show I always made sure he had good lines so he got big laughs, and every week there was a different actress playing his girlfriend. And they were all beautiful. But Ronnie still liked the Luau. So there was only one thing left for me to do: check out the Luau. And I did. I went there one night, and I must admit that the Luau did have something special—the noodles in the chow mein were really crisp.

FIFTY-THREE

F-F-F-Freddie Fox's writing partner, Seaman Jacobs, used to tell me about his amazing mother. Though she was past her ninety-sixth birthday, she was still bright, alert, and active. When people asked her her age she'd tell them ninety-six. Seaman would always add, "And a half."

His mother would get very annoyed at that. She'd say, "Seaman, stop it! Ninety-six is old enough!"

One day Seaman went shopping with her and they stopped at a store so she could buy some buttons.

"What do you want these for?" the salesgirl asked.

"I'm going to sew them on a sweater," his mother replied.

Amazed, the salesgirl said, "You mean you can still sew on buttons at your age?"

"You know she's ninety-six," Seaman said.

"And a half!" his mother added.

FIFTY-FOUR

I was never a great lover. When I was young, the only thing I wanted to get into was show business. Gracie and I had a wonderful marriage, but I can't remember ever getting applause for what I did in our bedroom.

I do remember this: After we'd been man and wife for about seventeen years, Gracie woke me up at two-thirty one morning. She said, "George, I can't sleep. Make me laugh."

So I made love to her, and she laughed.

FIFTY-FIVE

The Sunshine Boys gave me my first real acting role in movies. I played Al Lewis, one of the two squabbling ex-vaudeville partners. Walter Matthau played the other one. He was great to work with. The script by Neil Simon was great. Everything we filmed was great until we came to the place where the ex-partners are back together doing their famous doctor sketch on a TV special.

It was a broad, burlesquey piece and it worried me. As they were getting ready to shoot, I said to Walter—wait. I shouldn't tell this about myself. This is how Walter tells it:

George said to me, "Walter, this sketch won't work. The props are funny." I didn't see where that was so bad, but he said, "You can't play funny dialogue against funny props. People won't know whether to watch the funny props or listen to the funny dialogue. You better tell

Neil." I figured George might have a point, but Neil Simon's one of our great writers. I said, "You tell him." He said, "It'll sound better coming from you." And he called Neil over and said, "Walter has something to tell you." So I said, "Neil, the sketch won't work." He said, "What do you mean, the sketch won't work?" I said, "The dialogue's funny and the props are funny . . . and you can't mix funny dialogue with funny props." He said, "I don't buy that, Walter. The sketch stays the way it is!" And George said, "I'm with you, Neil."

Now you know why I didn't want to tell that one.

FIFTY-SIX

Of all the movies I've made, the only one that had me worried was the one that turned out to be my biggest hit with the critics as well as with the public. I'm talking about the first *Oh, God*! film.

When I heard that Warner Brothers wanted me to play God in the movie I was very excited. They had a great script by Larry Gelbart, Carl Reiner would direct it, and John Denver would be starring in it with me. It sounded great.

But the minute I accepted the role I started to worry. Should I be the one to play God? We're both about the same age, but we grew up in different neighborhoods. Maybe they'd be better off with someone like Billy Graham. He's taller than I am. If I played Him, what would be my attitude? My motivation? What kind of voice should I use? I was very confused, so I looked up and hollered, "How do you play God?!" But there was no answer.

Then, when they showed me the outfits

I'd be wearing for the role, I figured they didn't have any more confidence in me than I did. I was expecting white flowing robes and a halo or two. That stuff they were going to put me in must have cost about twelve cents. It looked like God was laying off.

The closer we got to the starting date, the more nervous I got. I lay awake at night, tossing and turning. "I should never have accepted the role. I'll be a flop. The critics will pan my every move." Then one night this thought occurred to me: What am I worrying about? I can't be criticized. Nobody has ever seen Him, so they won't know whether I played Him right or wrong, whether I was good or bad.

That changed my whole attitude. Now I couldn't wait to get started. In the week that still remained before shooting began I lived the part, rehearsing day and night, before dinner, after dinner, during dinner, while driving, while doing my exercises. I never stopped. I got so into the role that one night when I said my prayers, I realized I was talking to myself.

The day we finally started shooting the movie, any lingering doubts that I had disappeared. Everything felt right. John Denver was perfectly cast and a pleasure to work with. So was Carl Reiner, although every once in a while he'd take me aside and say, "Look, George, this scene isn't moving, it needs a little more God-stuff." Or, "George, we're going to do that scene over, it needs more Goddishness." Once he stopped a scene right in the middle to say, "Hold it, George, you read that speech all wrong. God would never say it that way."

"Look, Carl," I said, "the last time you had lunch with Him did he have any other suggestions?"

Carl paused for a second, then started to laugh. "Okay, George, do it your way."

Carl Reiner and I had a very delightful relationship. One day, just before lunch, he came up to me a little worried and said, "George, I'm in trouble. I'm supposed to speak at a luncheon today at the Sportsmen's Lodge, and I forgot my toupee. Can I borrow yours?"

"Of course, Carl, what are friends for?" So he put on my toupee and left. When he returned I asked him, "How did your speech go, Carl?"

"Your hair was a riot," he said.

FIFTY-SEVEN

This incident took place in New York one summer while I was filming *Going in Style*. It was Saturday, and I was having lunch at the Friars Club with Henny Youngman and Lawrence Welk. I took a look at the three of us and immediately ordered a double martini. After I drank it we didn't look any better.

Then Rudy Vallee came over, and I ordered another martini. The waiter brought it over, took a look at us, and drank the martini. Then he said, "What would you gentlemen like for lunch?" I said, "Four pacemakers and some coffee."

Anyway, after lunch I said, "You know, fellows, we're in the wrong end of show business. The kids nowadays have got it made with their records and their albums and their concerts. They're making a fortune. Every Sunday they give a concert in Central Park and they work to fifty or sixty thousand people. We ought to go there tomorrow. We might learn something.

Maybe some of that youth will rub off on us, and maybe some of what we've got might rub off on them. That is, if it doesn't drop off before we get there."

I finally convinced them, and the next day we all met in Central Park. Not to look conspicuous, we wore tight jeans, dirty white sneakers, open shirts, and long gold chains hanging down our necks. We didn't belong at that concert. We didn't even belong in Central Park. The park looked beautiful with all those flowers; the four of us looked like we hadn't been watered in sixty years.

We thought they might call on us to entertain, so Henny Youngman brought his violin, Lawrence Welk brought his accordion, and Rudy Vallee brought an orchestration of "Vagabond Lover" that was arranged for him by John Philip Sousa's father. And with that open shirt I didn't want to catch cold, so I wore the buckskin vest that Daniel Boone gave me for my bar mitzvah.

But you never saw such an audience. They screamed, they hollered, they whistled, they stood on the seats, they hugged each other, they danced up and down the aisles. Then the concert started.

By the finish, the four of us were a little tired, so we sat down on the grass. That took about twenty minutes. Rudy Vallee never made it, his jeans were too tight.

Now, at this concert some of the kids were smoking grass, so I thought I'd try it. I pulled out a handful of grass, pushed it into my cigar holder, and lit it. It was nothing. The fertilizer was murder!

Then Henny Youngman started to play his violin, Lawrence Welk played the accordion, and Rudy Vallee and I started to harmonize. Then the police came.

One cop said, "What's going on here? What have you fellows been drinking?"

I said, "Prune juice on the rocks."

He said, "You better break it up and get out of here before it gets dark."

I said, "But, Officer, it's only three o'clock in the afternoon. It doesn't get dark until eight."

He said, "By the looks of this group, it'll take you that long to get out of here."

So we broke it up, but the cop was wrong. It took us longer. We had to go back for Lawrence Welk. He couldn't get up. His gold chain was stuck in his zipper.

FIFTY-EIGHT

In one of my films they had a young bit player who was very pretty, but a terrible actress. However, she was very ambitious and decided that if she got some experience in the theater, it would help her career. Fortunately, she had a wealthy boyfriend who backed a road company of *The Diary of Anne Frank* just so she could play the leading role—Anne Frank.

Before the opening in Cleveland, Ohio, they had three weeks of intensive rehearsals, and every day was more and more frustrating for the director. The actress was impossible. She couldn't remember her lines, her delivery was amateurish, and the more she rehearsed, the worse she got. The director was ready to quit the show, but she told him she was a poor rehearser. "Believe me," she assured him, "when I face that opening-night audience, it'll all come together."

She invited me to the opening night, but I was not all that anxious to see her perform,

111

and I had even less desire to be in Cleveland in February. A friend of hers and mine did go, and later he told me what I'd missed.

When the curtain went up she blew her opening lines, and her performance went downhill from then on. By the intermission the audience was totally fed up with her. Then, in the first scene in the second act, when the Nazi soldiers broke into the home, overturning furniture and shouting, "Where is she? Where's Anne Frank?!" the whole audience yelled back, "She's in the attic!"

FIFTY-NINE

Lounge acts used to be very popular in Las Vegas. Many talented performers did them, but to me, the best of all was Shecky Green. He was a fixture at the Riviera Hotel lounge, packing them in night after night.

For a time I was making several appearances a year at the same hotel, so we saw a lot of each other. He often dropped into my dressing room before I went on. I looked forward to those visits. He was full of hilarious stories.

But one night he asked if I knew that Frank Sinatra saved his life. Well, I'd never heard that, so he told me how it happened.

In 1967 he was working with Frank at the Fontainebleau Hotel in Miami Beach. After a midnight show, he left the hotel by the back entrance, and when he stepped out into the dark alley, five guys jumped on him. He said, "They were beating the crap out of me. And then I heard Frank Sinatra say, 'That's enough!'"

Until those last two words I thought what Shecky was telling me really happened.

The next afternoon I passed the lounge just as Shecky was telling his audience, ". . . and then I heard Frank Sinatra say, 'That's enough!' " It got a two-minute laugh.

Now I wonder about all those hilarious stories in my dressing room. Maybe he was trying out his new material on me.

SIXTY

I once asked Red Skelton if it was true that before going onstage to perform he always threw up. He said, "Doesn't everyone?"

Coming from Red, that surprised me. It shouldn't have. Performers who seem the most confident often are the most insecure. And even with the ones who really have confidence, it may be only skin deep. One little setback and they are down for the count.

I know a Las Vegas comic, whose name I won't mention, who for years kept telling me I owed it to myself to catch his act. Well, I hate to owe anyone, even myself. So one night, when I was playing an engagement there, I decided to pay my debt.

By the time I got to his hotel he'd finished his act. I went backstage to at least say hello. When I stepped into his dressing room, there he was, holding court, surrounded by his claque of hangers-on.

I never heard such a rave review as the one he was giving himself. "How about that show! What a performance! What delivery! Sharp . . . with it . . . I had them eating out of my hand!"

A voice piped up, "I don't know . . . I didn't think you were that good."

And he said, "The band loused me up."

SIXTY-ONE

Joe E. Lewis was one of our greatest night-club performers. He was also one of show business's biggest gamblers. One night I was standing with him at the crap table at the El Rancho Hotel, where he was working, and I watched him lose thousands of dollars in a few minutes.

Then, when he told the pit boss to put five Gs on the hard ten, I had to open my mouth. I said, "Joe, you can't risk $5,000 on one bet!"

He said, "I can't? I just did."

I said, "Joe, it's crazy. You're throwing away everything you make. You just have to start saving for a rainy day."

"Oh, sure, sure," he said. "I'll save and save and save, and with my luck it won't rain and I'll be stuck with all that money."

SIXTY-TWO

I love Ann-Margret, not only because she's one of the nicest girls in show business, but because she always tells everyone that I discovered her.

When she was nineteen years old, I took her to Las Vegas to appear in my act during the holidays. On opening night she came off the stage and started to cry. I said, "Annie, why are you crying? The audience loved you."

She said it was Christmas Eve and she missed her mother. So I told her to go into my dressing room and phone her mother and charge it to me. Then I went out on the stage to entertain.

An hour later I went back to my dressing room and she was still on the phone. I sat there and waited until she was finished, then I said, "Annie, you're not crying anymore. Your mother was glad to hear from you, huh?"

She said, "Oh, yes, Mr. Burns. We had a wonderful conversation."

I asked her why she didn't invite her mother to Las Vegas, and she told me she couldn't, her mother lived in Sweden. Then *I* started to cry.

SIXTY-THREE

After Sammy Davis lost sight in one eye when he was in that automobile accident many years ago, he was afraid to drive a car.

Several years later, Joey Bishop, Sammy, and I were set to do a big benefit show in Las Vegas, and Sammy, who had overcome his fear by then, insisted that we let him drive us there in his car. We weren't on the freeway twenty minutes before I realized the kid not only lived fast, he drove fast. The motorcycle policeman behind us must have realized that, too, because a minute later, he pulled us over to the side of the road.

"I was only going sixty-five," Sammy said, before the cop could open his mouth.

"Sorry, buddy, you were doing eighty," the cop corrected him. "Why don't you keep your eye on the speedometer?"

Joey Bishop broke in. "Officer, the man has only one eye. Do you want him to watch the road or the speedometer?"

I was a little annoyed with Joey. He shouldn't have said that line about Sammy's eye. *I* should have said it.

SIXTY-FOUR

Ever since becoming a member of the Hillcrest Country Club, I've always sat at the same table when I have my lunch. It's called the "Round Table." The reason it's called the "Round Table" is because it's a table that's round. I feel that an author should throw in these bits of information now and then. On second thought, maybe this is one I should have thrown out.

Anyway, for many, many years, when you sat at the "Round Table" you would be surrounded by the biggest comedians in the business. There were the Marx Brothers—Groucho, Chico, and Harpo—the Ritz Brothers—Harry, Jimmy, and Al—Jack Benny, George Jessel, Danny Kaye, Al Jolson, Eddie Cantor, Lou Holtz, and sometimes a few more, each one trying to top the others. They're all gone. I sit alone at the "Round Table." Now I'm the funniest one there.

In the old days, Jessel was the funniest, to me at least. Even though Jack Benny was my closest friend, I can't say he was the funniest. He was the best audience, the one who made all the rest think they were the funniest.

With or without Jack Benny, Groucho thought he was the funniest. Sometimes maybe he was. Groucho had a very fast, caustic wit. He was loaded with great puns, and even more loaded with gall. If the right situation came up, he didn't mind repeating the same joke twenty times in one day.

Years ago, Sophie Tucker used to sing a song called "If You Can't See Mama Every Night, You Can't See Mama at All." Well, Groucho did a big job at the "Round Table" with that one. Every time I ordered sea bass, without fail Groucho would say, "If you can't sea bass every night, you can't sea bass at all." I laughed the first time he said it, but after hearing it for forty years it begins to lose its freshness.

One day I wanted to order sea bass for lunch, but Groucho was sitting at the table and I didn't want to hear that lousy joke again. So I took the waiter aside and I quietly whispered, "I'll have some sea bass."

And the waiter quietly whispered back,

"If you can't sea bass every night, you can't see bass at all."

After hearing that line again from the waiter I decided it was time to change my diet. I went back to the table and said, "Groucho, do you have any jokes about whitefish?"

He said, "No, George."

I turned to the waiter and said, "I'll have some whitefish."

And Groucho said, "If you can't see whitefish every night, you can't see whitefish at all."

I told you he had gall.

SIXTY-FIVE

Chico Marx loved to gamble. He spent most of his time and money at the track or at a bridge table.

Once, when the Marx Brothers were in San Francisco, he rushed over to a bridge club he'd been to before. When he got there, the place was empty, except for four fellows in the midst of a game. Since cutting in wasn't allowed, the only way Chico could get into their game was if one of the players quit.

So Chico took one of them aside and whispered, "You're being cheated. That guy in the blue suit, when he holds his cigarette on the left side of his mouth, that means he's got clubs. When he puts the cigarette in the center of his mouth, that means he's got diamonds. If it's on the right side, he's got hearts. And when he doesn't put the cigarette in his mouth at all, that means spades." The man thanked Chico profusely and quit the game, and Chico took his place, lost $1,200, and had a great afternoon.

SIXTY-SIX

Hardly a day goes by that I don't play bridge at my club. In the group I usually play with, we're all about the same age, all forgetful, and the other three are very hard of hearing.

One day, two of them forgot their hearing aids, and Artie, the third one, had his hearing aid but forgot the battery for it. I opened the first hand with a bid of one spade; the opponent to my left said a heart; my partner said one diamond; and the fourth guy said a club. I said, "Good-bye, gentlemen, we'll play tomorrow." And Artie said, "Thanks, George, and you look good, too."

A few days later I was playing with the same group. This time all three had their hearing aids, batteries and all, so they were really ready. Our opponents had a sensational hand and bid seven no-trump. Artie, who was my partner, had the lead and laid down the ace of spades, which of course took the trick and immediately set the hand. I said, "Artie, if you had the ace of spades, why the hell didn't you double?" And he said, "I was afraid they would go into another suit."

I said, "Thanks, Artie. And you look good, too."

SIXTY-SEVEN

Bridge is the only game I play. I gave up golf long ago. For years I tried it, but it wasn't for me. I was pathetic. Everyone I played with at the club was pathetic: Jack Benny, Danny Kaye, the Ritz Brothers, Georgie Jessel. But they took it seriously. I didn't. I only felt sorry for the pro, Eric Monti. He had to give us lessons.

Poor Jessel. He could never break 100. It was always 110 or 120. One day I was in the locker room, and he came in all excited, screaming that he'd just shot a 99. I asked him how he did it, and he said, "I'll tell you how I did it. Every shot was perfect."

Jack Benny was the most pathetic of all. I was on the green with him once and he missed his putt. When I say he missed it, I mean he didn't even hit the ball. He almost cried. He should have. Whoever heard of whiffing a putt?

Another time Jack and I were in a foursome with Gary Morton, who was Lucille Ball's husband at the time, and Jack's brother-in-law, Hilliard Marks. On the first tee, Jack's drive went about ten feet. Gary said, "That swing sounded good, Jack. Take another one." He swung again. Same result. I said, "Sounded good." His next shot off the fairway went no place. "Sounded good," we all said. By now he was furious. "Sounded good! Sounded good!" he shouted. "I'm playing golf, I'm not giving a concert!"

As bad as I played, I don't think I ever lost my temper on the golf course. It just wasn't that important to me. But it did aggravate me that I couldn't break a hundred, that I couldn't come home and tell Gracie I shot an 80. So one day I came home and told Gracie I shot an 80, and I felt better. That's when I found out I didn't have to play golf at all. I could play bridge and come home and say I shot an 80.

SIXTY-EIGHT

Do you remember Lou Clayton of Clayton, Jackson, and Durante? He started out as the dancer in their original act and later became the business manager. Durante and Jackson were both pussycats, but Lou, who was only about five feet six, had a hot temper, was tough as nails, and didn't take anything from anyone.

Well, one day we played golf together. He had a good first nine, but on the second nine he shanked a two-iron into the lake. It upset him so much that he picked up his big bag with all those beautiful clubs and threw them into the lake, too. I couldn't believe it. I said to him, "Lou, why do you play golf?"

And he said, "It relaxes me."

SIXTY-NINE

Jess Oppenheimer was one of the top comedy writers in radio and television. He was not only the producer and head writer of the "I Love Lucy" show from the very beginning of that TV series, but he also helped create it. Lucy was so happy with him that for their first Christmas together she bought him a gross of golf balls with his name, Oppenheimer, on each ball.

Every chance he had to get away from his work, Jess would be on the golf course, playing a fast eighteen holes with his Christmas golf balls. One day he hit a drive into the rough, saw it fall, and went after it. A golfer from the adjoining fairway had also hit a ball into the same rough, and by the time Jess got to his ball, his fellow was standing over it.

"This is my ball," the man said.

Jess said, "Oh, no, it's mine. I saw it fall right here."

"I'm sure it's my ball," the fellow said as he picked it up. "See, it *is* mine," he gloated. "It's an Oppenheimer."

SEVENTY

It's hard to believe, but there was a period in Al Jolson's life when his career was at a standstill. Suddenly, the "World's Greatest Entertainer" was old hat and the jobs weren't coming in.

At that time, sturgeon wasn't sold in California. And Jolson, who still had millions, was very fond of this delicacy. So every week he'd fly in $150 worth of sturgeon and keep it in the refrigerator at our country club.

I often had lunch with him, and one day I said to him, "Joley, to me you'll always be the greatest showman that ever lived." Beaming over my big compliment, he said, "Thanks, George. And how would you like a little sturgeon for lunch?" I said I'd love it, and it was delicious. After that, every time I saw Jolson, I paid him a compliment, and I had sturgeon for lunch. It got so I liked sturgeon more than I liked Jolson.

Then Columbia made *The Jolson Story*, an instant smash. Larry Parks played Jolson, but he didn't do the singing. It was Jolson who sang every song on the sound track, which became the hit of the movie. I saw the film and was thrilled. The next day, when I saw Jolson, I said, "Joley, I saw the movie and that sound track is the greatest thing I've ever heard."

Looking straight at me, he said, "You can buy your own sturgeon, kid. I'm a hit again."

SEVENTY-ONE

Of all the comedians I have known, George Jessel may not have been the most successful, but without a script he was the funniest. I'm not sure about this, but I think he also said "I do" the most often.

In all fairness, if his five weddings set a record, you'd have to put an asterisk after it, because three of those weddings were to the same woman, his first wife, Florence Courtney. When he met her, Florence was one of the Courtney Sisters, a popular singing act on the same vaudeville circuit he was playing.

In 1921, two years after their wedding, he divorced her. She must have had something going for her, because he had to remarry and divorce her twice more before he got her out of his system.

Georgie's next wife was the beautiful screen star Norma Talmadge. And finally, when he was in his forties, came wife number three, the sixteen-year-old starlet

Lois Andrews, who taught him how to play hopscotch.

The marriage to Norma Talmadge lasted the longest. He was crazy about her, but they quarreled constantly. Finally, one day she left him for a doctor in Miami, Florida. Jessel went out of his mind. He bought a gun, chartered a plane, flew to Miami, and went straight to her hotel. When she opened the door to her suite, there, beside her, was the doctor. Jessel pulled out his gun and took a shot at him. But instead of hitting the doctor, the bullet went through the window and wound up two blocks away—in the rear end of a gardener who was bent over, cultivating pansies.

When the gardener took Jessel to court, the judge asked, "Mr. Jessel, how is it possible for you to take a shot at someone ten feet from you and hit a gardener two blocks away?"

"Your Honor," Jessel answered, "I'm an actor, not Buffalo Bill."

SEVENTY-TWO

This one took place many years after the gardener incident.

One morning I was at my club, and I noticed that Jessel was already at the bar. After a few minutes I went over to him and said, "Georgie, I've been watching you. That's your third brandy and it's only nine o'clock in the morning."

"Didn't you know?" Jessel said. "Norma Talmadge left me."

"But she left you thirty years ago," I reminded him.

And Jessel said, "I still miss her."

SEVENTY-THREE

Here's another Sammy Davis story. When Sammy was an up-and-coming young performer, having gone out on his own from the Will Mastin Trio, Jerry Lewis, Jack Benny, and several other top entertainers helped him prepare a solo act. They gave him advice, plugged him into all the networks and studios, and heckled his agent to get him better jobs. Sammy was so grateful that he converted to Judaism.

As soon as Sammy became a star, he began spending fortunes on jewelry and clothes, and started a series of golf lessons. He bought the most expensive set of golf clubs and ten cashmere golf outfits.

When I heard that Sammy was interested in golf, I invited him to the Hillcrest Country Club to play a round with me. While we were waiting to tee off on the first hole, I asked him what kind of a handicap he had.

"The biggest," Sammy replied. "I'm a black, one-eyed Jew."

SEVENTY-FOUR

Did you know that Danny Kaye always wanted to be a doctor? Well, he did. He was fascinated by medicine. His idea of a good time was to fly to the Mayo Clinic and watch operations. You think I'm kidding? One day he asked me to go with him.

He said, "George, we'll have a great time. We'll see a couple of bypasses, a kidney transplant, a bowel resection. . . ."

It was very tempting, but I had a good excuse for not going—I wasn't interested.

I'll never forget when Danny and Sylvia Kaye gave a party some years ago. There were thirty or forty of us there, and after dinner a doctor who was one of the guests happened to mention a big flu epidemic going around and advised everyone to get flu shots. Well, that was all Danny had to hear. He made the doctor go out to his car and bring back his bag. Then we all had to roll up our sleeves, and while the doctor watched, Danny gave us the shots. And he did a pretty good job, too. I didn't catch the flu until I got home. I called Danny the next morning to find out what I should do about it.

He said, "George, this is Wednesday," and hung up.

SEVENTY-FIVE

When I was seventy-eight I had a triple bypass. I wasn't going to have it, but my manager, Irving Fein, made such a good deal for me I couldn't turn it down.

It was a tough negotiation. My doctor started off by claiming I had a heart condition. But Irving said, "Wait a minute. How do we know it's a heart condition? Maybe it's only a little indigestion that will go away in a few days."

The doctor answered, "If he's not operated on, *he'll* go away in a few days."

Well, we lost that point.

The doctor told me I'd be in the hospital for two or three weeks, but I didn't want a booking for that long. I'd never played the room before, and I wasn't sure about the acoustics. So Irving settled for a three-day tryout with an option to renew.

The doctor wanted me in a private room, but Irving decided a semiprivate room was good enough. Actually, I prefer a semiprivate room. As long as I'm lying there, I might as well have someone around to try out my routines on.

Well, we finally finished the negotiations: a package deal, including surgery. And I must say, Irving did a good job. He even got me top billing, right over Emergency Room.

And the operation was a success. We had a good audience watching from the observation room above. After the doctor completed the triple bypass, he got an ovation. In fact, he got so carried away, he was tempted to do a fourth bypass for an encore. Fortunately, Danny Kaye was standing next to him and talked him out of it.

I don't want to tell you what the final bill was, but maybe this will give you a little hint. One of my friends was in the hospital for two days straight and it cost him $2,600. And he'd come there only to visit me.

Oh, I forgot to tell you—while I was being operated on, Irving was up in the observation room selling autographed copies of my latest album.

SEVENTY-SIX

All in all, I've been pretty lucky with my health. In fact, after having my tonsils out when I was still in vaudeville, I didn't see another doctor for twenty years. Oddly enough, it was my throat again.

I had developed sort of a tickle in my throat, which caused me to constantly keep clearing it. It got so, I couldn't even finish a sentence without doing it. By then, I was married to Gracie, and with all this hacking of mine she couldn't get any sleep. Also, we were on the radio at the time, so I was not only annoying Gracie, I was annoying the whole country.

Anyway, I went to all the great doctors, every throat specialist I could find. They all looked into my throat and said the same thing: "Stop smoking!" So I stopped, and it got worse.

One day Abe Lastfogel—he was the head of the William Morris Agency—called me and said, "George, I heard you on the radio last night, and you better do something about that throat. If you keep hacking that way, the sponsor's never going to renew your contract."

I said, "Abe, I don't know what to do. I've been to every doctor in the country."

"George," Abe said, "you haven't been to Dr. Ginsberg. He runs a little eye, ear, nose, and throat clinic in downtown Los Angeles. He only charges three dollars a visit and he's a genius."

Well, I got down there as fast I could. When I went into his office there were about forty people in the waiting room. I went over to the nurse and said, "Would you tell Dr. Ginsberg that George Burns is sitting outside?"

She went into the other office, and a minute later she returned. She said, "I told Dr. Ginsberg that George Burns was sitting outside, and he told me to tell you that Dr. Ginsberg is sitting inside." So I sat down, hacked, coughed, cleared my throat, and waited my turn.

When I finally got into the doctor's office I kept hacking and hacking and hacking. He examined my throat and said, "What's your problem?"

I said, "What's my problem! Can't you tell? I keep making this hacking noise."

The doctor said, "Why do you do that?"

I sat there stunned. Nobody had ever asked me that question before. I said, "I don't know why I do it."

Dr. Ginsberg said, "Then if I were you, I wouldn't do it anymore."

And you know something—I never did.

SEVENTY-SEVEN

Goldie Hawn is a beautiful girl and a great actress, and I always enjoyed working with her. She guest-starred in one of my television specials, and her dressing room was right next to mine. There was a hole in the wall between our two rooms. I didn't cover it up. I figured, let the kid enjoy herself.

SEVENTY-EIGHT

Dean Martin had a deservedly high-rated weekly hour-long TV show that went on for years, but he paid absolutely no attention to it. Everything—the casting, the creative decisions, the scripts—was left to his director, Greg Garrison, and to Greg's staff.

The day the show was being taped before a studio audience was the first time Dean found out what he was supposed to do on it. He would come in about three hours before the taping began. Then, while the entire show was being rehearsed on the stage, Dean would sit in his dressing room with his head writer, Harry Crane, have a martini or two—or three—look at the monitor, and watch his stand-in go through all Dean's stuff. He stayed there until they called him out to start the show.

It was no accident that Harry Crane was allowed in Dean's dressing room. A veteran writer, Harry had a storehouse of gags and stories to amuse Dean with. He also had an instinct for coming up with just the right thing to say at the right time.

Once he was telling Dean about a singing trio he had just seen at one of the Las Vegas hotels. "You wouldn't believe the show they put on," he told Dean. "The worst. No voices. No technique. No relationship with each other. No rapport with the audience." On and on he went, lambasting their choice of songs, their lack of preparation, until finally Dean interrupted.

"I don't know," he said. "I saw that act two weeks ago, and I thought they were pretty good."

Without skipping a beat, Harry said, "You didn't let me finish."

SEVENTY-NINE

Of all the show-business drinkers around lately, Dean Martin is one of the best—or worst, depending on how you look at it.

The last time I saw Dean in a nightclub, he staggered out onstage with a glass of booze in his hand, turned to his piano player, and slurred, "How long have I been on?"

It got a big laugh. But actually that was Dean's standard opening. I don't know if Dean Martin drinks as much as he says he does, but I do know that his serious drinking is done when he's offstage, not when he's performing. He may have a shot or two while he's out there, but when he's working, he's far from potted.

However, Dean found out a long time ago that his whole act works best when the audience thinks he really is a bit tipsy. That's his image and he knows how to preserve it.

One night a woman jumped up on the stage, grabbed the glass out of Dean's hand, drank it, and said, "This isn't booze—you're drinking tea!" Dean looked at her and said, "Lady, you're drunker than I am."

EIGHTY

This one is about Judy Garland. I had been asked to speak at one of those big Hollywood testimonial dinners where all those who are going to be on the dais wait together in a reception room until all the guests have been seated at their tables. This night I was in the reception room, sitting with Judy Garland, and Sid Luft, whom Judy was married to at the time, took me aside and said, "George, you'll be sitting next to Judy on the dais, too, and you can do me a very, very big favor. Don't let her drink too much tonight because she has to sing."

I assured Sid I'd take care of it. When I went back to Judy, there on the table were two dry martinis. I quickly drank half of mine, and when she wasn't looking, I switched glasses. I did that in the reception room, and I did that when we were seated on the dais. I must have done it five or six times . . . maybe ten . . . I was so busy switching glasses I didn't have time to count.

About twenty olives later, George Jessel, who was master of ceremonies, introduced me, saying, "Ladies and gentlemen, and now George Burns!"

I looked around and couldn't find him. Milton Berle, who was also on the dais, came over and picked me up. "That's you, you're George Burns," he said. I just stood there and started to make my speech without even going to the microphone. Naturally, nobody heard me, which is just as well, since I wasn't making any sense. Milton quickly pushed me back into my seat, and Jessel explained to the audience, "George Burn's speech was written by that famous writing team of Haig and Haig."

Later Judy got up and sang "Over the Rainbow," and was a smash. She was over the rainbow, and I was under the table. On the way out, after the dinner was over, Sid Luft said to me, "George, you were disgusting tonight."

EIGHTY-ONE

To some people it's not the drinking they enjoy, it's the ritual that goes with it. Some years ago José Ferrer moved into Beverly Hills, and one night I dropped in at about nine o'clock to say hello. He asked me if I'd like a martini, and I said sure. Now, when I make a martini, I take an old-fashioned glass, fill it with ice, then fill it with gin, put in some vermouth, and in two seconds I've got a martini.

But not José. First he got a snifter glass big enough to swim in, took three jiggers of gin, and slowly rolled them down the side of the glass. Then he took an eyedropper filled with vermouth and carefully rolled two drops down the other side of the snifter. Then he took one ice cube and a spoon and gently lowered it into the glass so as not to bruise the gin. Then he took the snifter glass in both hands and rocked it back and forth until the cube of ice melted. I went home at eleven o'clock and he was still making that martini.

I went back to pay him a visit three months later, and he said, "George, can I make you a martini?"

I said, "I haven't got time, I'm booked to play Vegas in two weeks."

EIGHTY-TWO

They tell me drugs are very popular here in Hollywood. I wouldn't know. I've never used drugs—any of them. I'm afraid to take even a laxative more than two days in a row.

I was actually at one of those parties, but I didn't have any idea what it was. I was hardly in the door when one of the guests came up to me and said, "George, have you got any junk on you?"

I said, "No, I give it all to the Salvation Army." It was the first time I ever saw anyone with two heads look at me like I had three.

Later at dinner, this attractive young girl sitting next to me leaned over and said, "George, do you ever use uppers?"

I said, "What for? I've got my own teeth."

The woman on the other side of me started to laugh and said, "She's talking about those uppers and downers."

I said, "Oh, the Uppers and Downers? I've never seen them. Where are they playing?" They all thought I was trying to be funny. They didn't know I had never been to a party like that.

At the end of the meal, out came a bowl of white powder, surrounded by a lot of little silver spoons. Well, I like my coffee sweet, so I put in three or four spoonfuls. The next thing I knew, the host was showing me to the door. And you won't believe this—I was never invited back.

EIGHTY-THREE

Of all my appearances in England, the most exciting might have been in 1976, when I performed at the London Palladium. A Royal Gala Charity Concert attended by Her Royal Highness Princess Margaret, it was a very successful evening and raised a lot of money.

Following the concert, the producer ushered me up to the Royal Box to meet Princess Margaret. There were a number of people there, and seated in the center of the group was this charming lady. So I went up to her and said, "Your Highness, it's a pleasure for me to meet you. I'd curtsy, but if I got down, I wouldn't be able to get up again."

She laughed and said, "I'm sorry, Mr. Burns, I'm not Princess Margaret, I'm the lady-in-waiting."

Just then the princess came in. I turned to her and said, "Your Highness, it's a pleasure for me to meet you, and you just missed one of my big jokes."

The princess gave me a puzzled look, and as she sat down, she gestured for me to sit next to her. We had a very pleasant conversation, and then she said, "Mr. Burns, you sing so fast I practically missed the lyrics to your first song."

I said, "Your Highness, would you like to hear me sing it again?"

She said, "No, once is enough." I had a funny comeback, but I'm not topping a princess.

Well, a few minutes later the princess stood up, and I assumed that this was my cue to leave. As I said good-bye and started to go, she stopped me and whispered, "No, no, Mr. Burns, I'm supposed to leave first."

I quickly stepped aside, and she left. Then, as I started to leave again, the lady-in-waiting tapped me on the shoulder and said, "Mr. Burns, I'm supposed to leave next." After she left I sat down; I didn't want to start another war with England. I sat there until everybody had left. Finally an usher opened up the curtains to the box and said, "Mr. Burns, the theater is empty, and you can leave after I do."

EIGTHY-FOUR

During one of my many trips to London, I became friends with a very wealthy, yet very modest, Jewish chap named Hyman Goldfarb. On one visit, Hy told me that because of his large donations to charities through the years, the queen wanted to knight him, but he was going to turn it down.

"That's a great honor," I said. "Why would you turn it down?"

"Because during the ceremony you have to say something in Latin," he said. "And I don't wish to bother studying Latin just for that."

"So say something in Hebrew. The queen wouldn't know the difference."

"Brilliant," Hy complimented me, "but what should I say?"

"Remember that question the son asks the father on the first night of Passover? . . . 'Why is this night different from all other nights?' Can you say that in Hebrew?"

"Of course," he said. "*Ma nishtana ha*

leila hazeh. Thank you, old sport. I shall become a knight."

At the ceremony Hy waited his turn while several of the other honorees went before the queen. Finally they called his name. He knelt before Her Majesty, she placed her sword on one shoulder and then on the other, and motioned for Hy to speak.

Out came *"Ma nishtana ha leila hazeh."*

The queen turned to her husband and said, "Why is this knight different from all other knights?"

EIGHTY-FIVE

Like many performers, I'm constantly being interviewed, and you'd be amazed at how many times I have to answer the same kinds of questions.

A few years ago I got a phone call from a newspaperwoman. She said, "Mr. Burns, is it true you go out with young girls?"

I said, "It's true."

She said, "Is it true that you smoke ten or fifteen cigars a day?"

I said, "It's true."

She said, "Is it true that you drink three or four martinis a day?"

I said, "It's true."

She said, "What does your doctor say?"

I said, "He's dead."

EIGHTY-SIX

I keep hearing from my young colleagues, like Milton Berle, Henny Youngman, and Sid Caesar, that these days it's a different kind of show business. Everything now is sex and nudity. They're not complaining, mind you, they're just stating facts.

When I was young, things were different. I remember playing the Chicago World's Fair in the 1930s. I was on the same bill with Sally Rand. She did her famous fan dance, and it was supposed to be very, very naughty. But it was nothing.

She came out on the stage wearing flesh-colored leotards, and the lights on the stage were dark blue—you could hardly see her. And when she did her fan dance, her fans were so big, they covered her completely. That was it.

She got sick one night, so I took her place and nobody knew the difference.

EIGHTY-SEVEN

Here's one that makes me laugh every time I think of it. A few years ago I thought I'd entertain my seven-year-old great-grandson with a funny incident that happened to Gracie. But it got kind of long and involved, and after I'd gone on and on for a while, he finally interrupted me.

"Grampa," he said, "get to the bottom line!"

EIGHTY-EIGHT

I think most performers appreciate it when total strangers take the time to say a complimentary word or two. I know I do. But once in a while, they'll come out with something that leaves you more annoyed than grateful.

Even though it had to be more than sixty years ago, I still remember this one. Gracie and I had been on the radio for just a couple of weeks, and we were walking down Broadway when a man stopped us. "Aren't you Burns and Allen?" he asked. We said we were, and he continued, "I heard you last night all the way from Cleveland," and he walked away. Gracie and I exchanged looks, and just then the man came back and added, "I can also get Philadelphia on my radio." I said, "Thank you, that's quite a compliment."

Once, when Gracie and I were spending an evening with Jascha Heifetz, one of the world's greatest violinists, he told us of an experience he had had in Akron, Ohio. He was giving a concert there, but that night there was a terrible storm and only about twelve people showed up. So the manager walked out and said he was very sorry, but Mr. Heifetz wouldn't appear that night and they would be refunding everybody's money. Well, this one fellow went backstage and said, "Mr. Heifetz, I'm one of your biggest fans. My wife and I drove all the way from Youngstown to see you. Couldn't you at least sing one song for us?"

EIGHTY-NINE

Several years ago, I came up with an idea for a publicity stunt that I thought was tremendous. I was sure it would break into newspapers all over the country. Everybody always kids me about my singing, so I decided to take advantage of it and insure my voice for a million dollars. A brilliant idea, wasn't it?

I was so excited I couldn't wait to rush down to the insurance company, and I took a cassette and a tape recorder with me so the insurance man could hear my voice. I explained to him that I wanted to insure my voice for a million dollars and I played my cassette for him. It was one of my best numbers: a syncopated version of "Yankee Doodle Blues" with a yodeling finish. He sat there and listened patiently to the whole thing, then he just looked at me and said, "Mr. Burns, you should have come to us before you had the accident."

This kid made me kind of nervous. That was a very funny line and I couldn't think of a way to top it. But it didn't dull my enthusiasm any; I kept right on punching. I said, "Look, this is my natural way of singing, and you don't have to worry about having to pay any claims. Whatever is going to happen to my voice has already happened."

He sighed and said, "Mr. Burns, we're talking about a million-dollar policy. I could understand if you sang like Crosby, Sinatra, or Tony Bennett. They have trained voices."

I said, "Okay, so mine isn't even house-broken. But let me tell you the truth. This whole idea is a publicity stunt. I take out this big policy, it breaks in all the papers, I pay the first premium, and then we cancel."

He shook his head and said, "Mr. Burns, you're wasting your time. If my boss heard that cassette with that yodeling finish, there's no way in the world he'd approve the policy."

"I'll make a deal with you," I said. "If your boss doesn't okay that policy, I'll buy you a new suit of clothes."

He shrugged and took the cassette into the next office. Five minutes later he came out and said, "Mr. Burns, make that a blue suit with double vents in the jacket and dark blue piping on the lapels."

Well, I never got the policy, but to show you what a sweet man I am, I threw in a monogrammed handkerchief for his breast pocket.

NINETY

When you're born, you start out life with two things: diaper rash and relatives. Both can be very annoying, but you can get rid of the rash. There's nothing worse than the relative who comes for a fun visit and is still there five years later.

In my family, when I was growing up, there was no such thing as relatives moving in. We didn't have room for them. We didn't have room for us. And if any of us left home, there was no coming back.

I'll never forget when my sister Teresa was married to Charlie Kalendar. They had a big fight and she showed up at the house one day. She said, "Mama, I'm teaching Charlie a lesson. I'm moving in with you."

My mother said, "If you really want to teach him a lesson, you go home and *I'll* move in with you."

My mother was something. She was ready for any emergency.

NINETY-ONE

My brother Sammy and his wife, Sarah, had a problem with her brother. It was a simple problem. Joe had been living with them for seven years, and they were sick of him.

One day Sammy figured out a way to get rid of Joe once and for all. "Tonight at dinner," he explained to Sarah, "we'll get into a big argument over the soup. I'll say it's cold . . . you'll say it's hot. If your brother agrees with me, you'll throw him out, and if he agrees with you, I'll throw him out."

She said, "Great!"

That night at dinner, Sammy said, "I can't eat this soup, it's ice cold!"

Sarah said, "It is not. It's warm as toast!"

Sammy said, "What are you talking about? I could skate on it!"

She said, "You're crazy, I just burned my mouth!"

They kept screaming at each other until

finally Sammy said, "Joe, is the soup hot or cold?"

And Joe said, "I'm not answering, I'm staying another seven years."

NINETY-TWO

I had seven sisters and four brothers, but the one I usually talked about in my stage show and TV specials was my sister Goldie. Not the real, lovable, conservative Goldie, but a Goldie that we created to get laughs. Our Goldie was not what I would call a loose woman, she was what I would call a *very* loose woman.

For example, at a point in my stage act, I would say to the audience, "Here's a couple of songs written by a piano player who worked in a house of ill repute. And the only ones who knew the songs were the girls who worked there—ladies of the evening. My sister Goldie taught me the songs."

A little later I would say, "There's one thing I'd like to clear up. My sister Goldie did not work in a house of ill repute . . . she owned it."

That was typical of the way we portrayed Goldie. And as long as the laughs continued, we stayed with it.

One day I got a call from my sister Mamie. When she said she wanted to talk to me about Goldie, I thought, Here comes the lecture. I said, "What about Goldie?"

She said, "You're always doing those off-color stories about Goldie, and I don't think it's right."

"Mamie," I said, "I just do that to get laughs. Why is that so wrong?"

"Because I'm your sister, too," Mamie said. "Why can't you do those stories about me for a change?"

NINETY-THREE

I don't suppose many of you are old enough to remember Gus Edwards. But you do remember "Round and round she goes, and where she stops, nobody knows." Sure you do—that was "Major Bowes and His Amateur Hour," every week on your radio.

Well, Gus Edwards was the Major Bowes of vaudeville. Gus would find talented kids, develop their acts, and send them around the vaudeville circuits. Jessel, Cantor, Berle, Phil Silvers, Walter Winchell, and lots of others got their start with Gus Edwards.

One night at the Friars Club, maybe fifteen, maybe twenty years ago, Jessel got into a political argument with some hothead who got more and more excited, until he finally pointed his finger at Jessel and screamed, "Your people killed Christ!"

"Well, I had nothing to do with it," Jessel said. "I was with Gus Edwards."

Only Jessel could come up with a line like that.

NINETY-FOUR

Everyone has little quirks that are hard to account for. That is, everyone but me. I don't have any quirks, big or little. I'm positive of that. Some people would say that in itself is a quirk.

Milton Berle had a manager named Danny Welkes, who told me about a quirk of Milton's that he could never understand.

Milton would say to him, "Danny, there's something important we have to discuss. Call me tonight at 9:42." Danny would call him at exactly 9:42. The next night it would go like this: "Danny, something's come up. Call me at 10:18 tonight." Danny would call at 10:18. When they were through, it would be, "Danny we have to talk further on this. Get back to me at 11:02." It went on like this for months—never, "Get back to me at your convenience," or "as soon as you can," or "tomorrow," or "this evening," or "around midnight." It was always to the minute. And that was exactly when Danny called.

One night Milton told Danny to call him at 10:46 the next morning. In order to do that, Danny had to break a dentist's appointment. But when the time came, he didn't get around to calling Milton's number until 10:49. He heard the phone picked up at the other end, and then Milton's voice saying, "Hello, stranger."

NINETY-FIVE

Someone once said, You know you're old when you bend over to tie your shoelaces and you say to yourself, "What else can I do while I'm down here?"

Another indication that you're old is when you have to quote someone else's funny line to start a story. I just did that, but I didn't have to. I could have started by stating that you've reached old age when each of your birthdays starts getting more and more attention. For me, that began with my eightieth birthday. The cards and presents took a big jump on that one.

One of the nicest presents I got came from Danny and Rosie Thomas. It was a beautiful silk Japanese kimono with a dragon all over the back. I sent them a note, which Danny told me they promptly framed and kept on a table in their living room.

This is what the note said: "Dear Danny and Rosie: Thanks so much for that beautiful kimono. It looked so good on me that when a girlfriend came over the next night,

I couldn't wait to model it for her. I told her I'd be right down, quickly put on the kimono, and stopped halfway down the stairs to pose for her. She said, 'Wow!'

"Then I opened the kimono . . . and she put on her hat and coat and went home."

NINETY-SIX

Abe Lastfogel ran the William Morris Agency forever, but he was just a little man, about five feet two inches. He wanted people to look up to him, so whenever it was possible, he would hire young agents his height or less. If his career ever bottomed out, Mickey Rooney knew he would always have a place to go. I was a client of the agency for many years, and when I visited their offices I felt like a giant.

At one of the William Morris Christmas parties they invited all their motion-picture, stage, and television stars, and we all mingled with the little agents and their wives. In the middle of the party, one of the agents rushed over to Abe Lastfogel's table with his young son in tow.

"Abe," he said, "this is my son. When he graduates from high school I'd like him to get a job at the agency. He's only fourteen, and look how short he is already."

ANOTHER
AUTHOR'S NOTE

This book could be my 100 best Jack Benny stories. I have that many. But maybe I'll just skip them altogether. I've told them 100 times. Besides, they all had the same finish: Jack on the floor, laughing his head off. That's not true. Some of them ended up with Jack in the street, laughing his head off.

I just changed my mind. Since no collection of my best stories would be complete without at least a few of those Benny gems, I've picked out a few to tell you now.

Jack laughed at anything I did. He even laughed when I did nothing. Like the time we were seated in a restaurant waiting to order, and after a minute went by Jack started laughing. I said, "What are you laughing at? I didn't say anything." And, barely able to get the words out, Jack said, "But you didn't say it on purpose."

What broke Jack up even more than that sort of thing was when I did something unexpected to

181

him, like noticing him on the street as I drove by, stopping the car, rolling down the window, calling him over, and when he got to the car, rolling up the window and driving away.

What broke him up the most was when I baited him into saying or doing something he didn't want to say or do. That's what really put him away, what made him laugh the hardest. It's out of all the stories where I do that to Jack that I've picked the ones to tell you now. So here they are—what I consider my funniest Jack Benny stories.

NINETY-SEVEN

With Jack, the last thing that happened to him was always the greatest. One day at our club he said, "George, I've just had the coldest glass of water I've ever had in my life!" Another time he said to me, "I just ate the most delicious bacon-and-tomato sandwich I ever tasted!" Once he interrupted me in the middle of a bridge game to tell me that Sammy, in the locker room, had just given him the greatest shoeshine he had ever had in his life.

I usually ignored these earthshaking discoveries of Jack's, but once in a while he'd come up with something you just couldn't walk away from. One Sunday morning Jack and I were having breakfast together at the club. After we gave our order, Jack said to me, "I was with the world's greatest comedian last night."

"Who were you with?" I asked him.

Jack sensed that he was heading for trouble. He hemmed and hawed, and finally said, "Well . . . you might not think he's the world's greatest comedian."

From Jack's attitude I knew he had put his foot in it, so from there on I started playing with him. I said, "Well, maybe this fellow isn't the world's greatest comedian— maybe he's the world's second-greatest comedian. Who is he?"

Jack said, "George, look—it was what he said last night that made him sound like the world's greatest comedian."

"Jack, what did he say?"

Fighting for his life, Jack stammered, "Well . . . it . . . it . . . it isn't *what* he said, it's how he said it."

Taking dead aim, I said, "Jack, you're one of the great comedians, and you've got a great delivery. Tell me the line, and if he made you laugh, I'm sure you'll make me laugh."

Jack said, "George, the line wouldn't be funny now. It was the situation last night that made the line funny."

I said, "Jack, I still would like to know who this great comedian is."

There was this long pause. Then, without daring to look at me, Jack said, "Larry Adler."

Now it was my turn to take a long pause.

Finally I said, "Larry Adler, the harmonica player, is the world's greatest comedian?"

Trying to dig his way out, Jack said, "George, let me tell you exactly what happened. Last night we went to a party, and the entrance to the house was this big, heavy iron gate. Well, Larry Adler went through first, and as I came through, that's when he said, 'Jack, don't slam the door.'"

I looked straight at him and said, "He must have said something else."

Irritably, Jack snapped. "That's it, George—'Don't slam the door'!"

I said, "And that line made you think that this harmonica player was the world's greatest comedian? 'Don't slam the door'? Jack, if I were you, I wouldn't go around telling people that Larry Adler said that line. It might not be his. Maybe he stole it from Borrah Minnevitch!" I could have worked on Jack for another few minutes, but by this time he was rolling on the floor laughing.

NINETY-EIGHT

Before we both were married, Jack and I used to eat together almost every night. Now, eating with Jack was an experience I'll never forget. He never liked what he ordered, he only like what you ordered. One night we were sitting in a restaurant, and he ordered a steak and I ordered roast beef. When our food came, he looked at my roast beef and his mouth started to water. He said, "George, would you like a piece of my steak?"

I said, "No. Then you'll want a piece of my roast beef."

Don't ask me why, but that struck him as funny and he laughed so hard he fell off his chair twice.

The next night we were in the same restaurant, and Jack said, "George, your roast beef looked so delicious last night I'm going to order it."

I said, "Good," and I ordered steak.

When our food came, he took a look at my steak and his mouth started to water.

He said, "George, would you like a piece of my roast beef?"

I said, "No, because then you'll want a piece of my steak."

This time he fell off the chair only once, because he'd heard that joke before.

Then, the following night, he ordered chicken and I had pot roast. He looked at my pot roast and his mouth started to water.

I said, "Hold it, you like pot roast?"

He said, "I love it." I gave him my pot roast and took his chicken. He looked at my chicken and his mouth started to water. I got up and went to the men's room. It was making me nervous getting laughs with that kind of material. When I came back Jack wasn't there. I asked the waiter, "Did Mr. Benny leave?"

The waiter pointed and said, "No, he's right there, under the table."

NINETY-NINE

Here's something I did at a party one night and it made Jack hysterical. You're not going to believe this, and I don't blame you because I still don't believe it, either. It started while we were both standing at the bar having a drink. We were wearing dinner clothes, and I noticed that there was a little piece of white thread stuck on the lapel of Jack's coat. I said, "Jack, that piece of thread you're wearing on your lapel tonight looks very smart. Do you mind if I borrow it?" Then I took the piece of thread from his lapel and put it on my lapel.

That was it—that was the whole thing. I'm not sure, but I think that during my life in show business I must have thought of a funnier bit—I certainly hope so. But that bit of business took Jack apart. He laughed, he pounded the bar, he kept pounding the bar, and finally he collapsed on the floor, laughing.

The next day I got a little box, put a piece of white thread in it, and sent it over to

Jack's house with a note that said, "Jack, thanks for letting me wear this last night."

A little later I got a phone call from Mary. She said, "George, that piece of white thread got here an hour ago and Jack is still on the floor. When he stops laughing I think I'll leave him!"

ONE HUNDRED

I did lots of bad things to Jack at parties, but maybe the worst thing I did to him was at one of his own parties.

Now, on the stage Jack was full of confidence. He never thought for a second that he wouldn't do well. But the minute he and Mary gave a party he was a nervous wreck, which means Jack was nervous once every twelve years. That's not true—Jack and Mary gave a lot of parties, and they were always great. But Jack constantly worried that his guests weren't having a good time.

Well, Gracie and I were at this one party of theirs. There must have been 150 people there, all having a fine time, talking and drinking and laughing, when sure enough, Jack took me aside and said, "George, the party's not moving."

I said, "Jack, it's moving. Look around, everybody's having a wonderful time."

"Stop buttering me up," he said. "I'm in show business, too, you know. I've played for audiences all my life, and this party is just lying there!"

I said, "Jack, you want this party to really move? Go upstairs, take off your pants, put on one of Mary's hats, and come down in your shorts playing the violin."

You won't believe this. He said, "Great idea," and up he went.

I turned to the guests, and in a hushed voice called for attention. "Ladies and gentlemen, our host, Mr. Jack Benny, star of stage, screen, and television, has gone upstairs and will be coming down in his shorts wearing a lady's hat and playing his violin. Just ignore him."

Down came our star doing his act, and nobody paid any attention to him. It finally dawned on Jack that I had been putting him on. He fell on the floor laughing, everyone else laughed, and while he was still on the floor, he looked up at me and said, "*Now* the party's moving."

YET ANOTHER
AUTHOR'S NOTE

That's 100 stories. There's an old expression in show business: "Always leave them wanting more." At the risk of having you readers say that I left you wanting less, I'm going to give you a couple of bonus stories.

If you don't like them, don't complain. They're free. If you do like them and feel guilty about getting something you didn't pay for, you can send me a dollar for each story. Don't forget, I have to support my mother and father.

ONE HUNDRED ONE

My good friend Carol Channing was very close to Alfred Lunt and Lynne Fontanne, who were known as the "King and Queen of the American Theater." They were married and usually worked together on Broadway in hit after hit before finally retiring to a farm in Wisconsin. Lynne told Carol this story about their reactions to the first film they made in Hollywood, *The Guardsman*, based on their Broadway play.

They both were very nervous when they went to see the first running of the film in the projection room, and when they returned home, she asked her husband how he liked her performance, and she asked him to be very blunt.

"You were wonderful," Lunt raved. "You looked beautiful, your voice had such power and depth, your eyes were luminous, and I think it was your best acting performance ever."

"Oh, thank you, dear, I'm so glad you feel that way."

"I certainly do. Now tell me, what did you think of my performance?" he asked.

"I thought you were brilliant," she answered. "You've never been better in anything you've done. Your lips looked a little thin, but your face was so handsome, I fell in love with you all over again. I practically cried at the emotion you produced in some of your scenes. I loved everything you did in the film."

Lunt thought for a moment, and then said, "Thin lips, eh?"

ONE HUNDRED TWO

This is a Jack Benny story that I've never told before. There are two reasons why I've never told it before: The first reason is that it's not a typical Jack Benny story. It doesn't end up with Jack falling down in a helpless laughing fit. The second reason I've never told this story before is that I'm not in it. Or maybe that's the first reason.

Anyway, here's the story. Jack had agreed to make an appearance at a big benefit show in Denver. For something like that he always liked to be there a day ahead of time. So the night before the show he flew from Los Angeles to Denver with Irving Fein, who was Jack's manager before he became my manager.

After checking into the Brown Palace Hotel and cleaning up a bit in their room, they went down to the lobby with the whole evening still ahead of them. They checked the newspaper, but there were no movies that they wanted to see. Jack, who was very gregarious and knew people in practically every city in the country, phoned a couple of his Denver friends, but they weren't home. What to do? They had already had their dinner and they didn't feel like eating another one.

Just when they were resigned to sitting around the lobby for the rest of the evening, they noticed a sign that said Oscar Levant was giving a piano concert that very night. What a break!

The concierge managed to get them two tickets in the third row center. Jack couldn't believe his luck. Oscar Levant was not only one of the wittiest people around, but he was a brilliant pianist. No one played Gershwin better than Oscar Levant.

Unfortunately, Oscar was subject to violent mood swings and long periods of deep depression. His wife, June, put him in so many institutions that he called her "committing June." When he was well, no one could be more entertaining. I know, because Gracie and I spent many evenings together with the Levants and the Bennys.

Just as Jack and Irving were about to leave for the concert hall, who should come walking through the lobby but Oscar Levant. When they stopped him, Oscar said, "What are you two doing here?"

"We're going to your concert, that's what we're doing here," Jack told him, beaming over the good news. "And we're in the third row center!"

"Jack, you can't go to the concert," Oscar said.

"What?"

"You can't go to the concert," Oscar repeated. Evidently what was good news to Jack wasn't good news to Oscar.

"But, Oscar," Jack started to protest.

"Don't 'but, Oscar' me. I'll see you sitting there and I'll be a nervous wreck. I won't be able to play a note."

"That's ridic—"

"Jack, I'm warning you—if I see you there, I'll never speak to you again!" With that, Oscar stomped off and left the two of them looking at each other.

This time Jack couldn't believe his bad luck. He was totally deflated. Finally he said to Irving, "Why don't you go? He didn't say you couldn't go to the concert." But Irving didn't want to go without Jack. He went to return the tickets, but the concierge told him they were non-returnable.

That may have bothered Irving, but it didn't bother Jack. What bothered Jack was that they spent the next two hours sitting in the lobby bored to tears. They were about to give up and go to their room when Oscar, back from the concert, came up to Jack and snarled, "Some friend! Where the hell were you?!"

A FINAL NOTE

Well, that's it. The book is finished, and I feel just as good as I did a month ago, when I started it.

Before I sign off, I want to thank my literary agents, Richard and Arthur Pine, for prodding me into undertaking this project; Phyllis Grann and her senior editor at Putnam, Christine Pepe, for their faith in the ability of a hundred-year-old former comedian to complete the job; Jack Langdon, my office manager and secretary of thirty-five years, for typing all these pages; and most of all, Irving Fein and Hal Goldman. Without their tremendous help, I'd still be on page three.

George Burns

Oh, by the way, I have a new nurse. The other one left. She's suing me for sexual harassment.

IF YOU HAVE ENJOYED READING
THIS LARGE PRINT BOOK AND
YOU WOULD LIKE MORE
INFORMATION ON HOW TO
ORDER A WHEELER LARGE PRINT
BOOK, PLEASE WRITE TO:

WHEELER PUBLISHING, INC.
P.O. BOX 531
ACCORD, MA 02018-0531